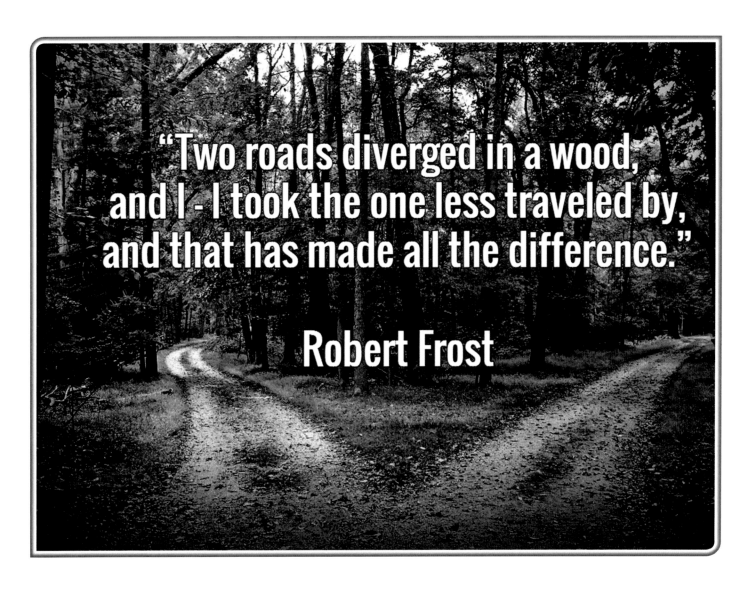

"Two roads diverged in a wood, and I - I took the one less traveled by, and that has made all the difference."

Robert Frost

Incredible Journey

ROBERT BRIAN HUNSAKER

AuthorHouse™
1663 Liberty Drive
Bloomington, IN 47403
www.authorhouse.com
Phone: 833-262-8899

This book is printed on acid-free paper.

ISBN: 979-8-8230-3048-9 (sc)
ISBN: 979-8-8230-3049-6 (e)

Library of Congress Control Number: 2024915358

Print information available on the last page.

Published by AuthorHouse 09/10/2024

authorHOUSE®

CHAPTER INDEX

FORWARD

This book is dedicated to Howard Lee Weatherly, and Billy Charles Vaden, my
best buddies in school, and who share the same birthday - November 10th.
Many of the people mentioned in the book are either deceased or gave permission
to use their names. Otherwise, the names were purposely omitted.

In Memoriam

Billy Charles Vaden ~ August 2023
Sharon Drake Weatherly ~ December 2023

PREFACE

For most of my adult life I've wanted to be a writer. But I never could think of a good story, nor did I have the discipline to sit down and write. I was always occupied with other activities. Finally, after sixty years, and comments from several friends, I realized I didn't need to create a story. I already had one – my own life adventures. My incredible journey, as I refer to it. It has been exciting, oftentimes humorous, and at times, somewhat dangerous. At least that's what friends tell me. All I really had to do was put it on paper. So ... here goes. I hope you enjoy my *"Incredible Journey"*.

1

CHAPTER

The Journey Begins

It started in the afternoon of November 10, 1939. Mom and Dad were in the maternity ward of the Methodist hospital in Dallas, Texas, awaiting my arrival. Probably, if they had known at the time what a renegade, I would turn out to be, they would have been someplace else. From an early age, I was always curious about anything new and different. I wanted to try anything and everything. The old saying, "curiosity killed the cat" maybe true, but the flip side - "he's as lucky as a cat with nine lives" may also apply. Fortunately, I fell into the latter category. We lived in a small brick home in north Dallas. Dad was born in Plainview, in the Texas panhandle in 1907. The family moved to Dallas when he was eleven years old. My paternal grandfather passed away before I was born. Dad had two sisters, and a younger brother, and being the oldest son, he became the family provider for his mother and siblings. This was during the "depression" days in the early 1930s.

My mother, Grace (Erwin) Hunsaker, had two older sisters, an older brother and a younger brother. The Erwin family moved to Dallas while she was still in school. Prior to the start of WWII, one of Mom's nephews was working for the FBI as an administrative assistant to J. Edgar Hoover, the long-time FBI director. On that infamous morning of December 7 in 1941 the Pearl Harbor base commander, Admiral Husband Kimmel, placed two calls to Washington. The first was to President Roosevelt advising the military base had been attacked by Japan. The second call was to the FBI for national security purposes. Mom's nephew, Ira K. Higby, was sitting by the phone and answered the call from Admiral Himmel and immediately alerted Director Hoover. Ironically, my cousin was the second person in the United States to learn of the attack on Pearl Harbor.

In 1932, Dad started a trucking business - "Hunsaker Trucking Contractor", which specialized in hauling oil field pipe and heavy equipment. The company was licensed by the regulatory authorities in 14 states, including Alaska. In the late 1950s oil and gas drilling had severely declined, so Dad switched to leasing trucks and trailers to major companies and changed the company name to "Hunsaker Truck Lease". Although he never finished high school, Dad had common sense with an ability to read situations. As a youngster instead of playing football or basketball, Dad was an accomplished gymnast specializing in the "flying rings" and the "parallel bars". In 1931 he won the Southern AAU Championship in New Orleans in the parallel bars and placed second in the flying rings, qualifying him for the 1932 Olympics, which was to be held in Los Angeles the following year. At this time, athletes receive no financial assistance. An athlete was responsible for his own travel expenses and lodging. With a wife and house payment, Dad could not afford to travel to Los Angeles, and therefore was unable to participate in the 1932 Olympics. However, a chance fortuitous meeting happened while Dad was working out at his local gym. One of his athletic skills was being able to balance on his hands and walk upside down. He was observed by a youngster present in the gym, who was apparently fascinated by this feat. He walked over to Dad and asked if he could teach him to stand on his hands. Dad agreed and in short order, successfully taught the young boy to stand and walk on his hands.

Prior to starting his own trucking company, Dad had been working at a local warehouse and delivery company for minimum hourly wages loading trucks. But he really wanted to get into sales, where his pay would be based on a commission, rather than an hourly rate. However, Dad's boss would never entertain the idea, since he didn't have a high school education. After Dad taught the young man to stand on his hands, he asked him his name and where he lived. The boy told Dad his name and an address in a prestigious neighborhood full of bank presidents and corporate board chairmen. When Dad asked what his father did. The boy replied, "He's the president of Dr. Pepper Bottling Company". A few days later, Dad received a call from the young man's father, thanking him for taking the time to help his son and asking what he could do to repay him? Dad replied that he didn't expect any payment, and that he just wanted to help his son. Dad told the father he worked at a local warehouse and delivery company and asked if they could handle some of the Dr Pepper delivery business. The father said he would instruct his warehouse manager to begin using Dad's company for local deliveries. The next day at work, Dad again approached his boss and asked if he could move to the sales department. As usual, the boss refused Dad's request. Whereupon Dad said, "What if I can get the Dr. Pepper Bottling account? Dad's boss laughed and replied, "You think you can get the Dr. Pepper business?" Little did he know that it was already a "done deal". Dad was transferred to the sales department, and his career in selling transportation was off and running. Since then, when Dad was asked how he got his start in the trucking business he would reply, "I taught a young man to stand on his hands." You can imagine the puzzled looks.

In 1932, Dad was approached by two brothers he knew who said they had a business proposition for him. It was regular trips hauling used furniture between Dallas and Houston. The brothers already owned a truck, but they needed a suitable trailer, and they asked Dad if he was interested in a partnership in the venture. Dad managed to borrow the money for a trailer using his Ford Model A as collateral. For the next several years, Dad solicited the freight, and the brothers made the weekly runs between Dallas and Houston, hauling used furniture. Dad passed away in 1981 at the age of 74. In 2006, more than seventy-five years after my father started Hunsaker Trucking Contractor, the family sold the company to a national trucking conglomerate for 28 million dollars. At the time of the sale, the company had 75 full time customers, 100 employees and over 1000 trucks and trailers, operating throughout the US from three terminals in Texas.

(My father Robert B Hunsaker, circa 1960)

("Flying H" - the Hunsaker Truck Lease logo)

When I was 2 ½ years old, we moved to a small ranch 5 miles northeast of Carrollton, Texas. The house was built in the late 1800s by a German immigrant and was a colonial 2 story with outside stairs leading to the bedrooms and bathrooms on the second floor. It was built on a foundation consisting of several large oak stumps sunk into the ground, typical for that era. The living room, dining room, kitchen, and a screened-in breezeway were on the ground floor. A full width patio extended across the front of the house. The property included a barn, and two small frame houses. Dad employed a ranch hand who, along and his wife, lived in one of the small houses.

(Bar B H Ranch, circa 1955; This picture was a Xmas card for several years.)

Dad's passion was horses and cattle. Most of the horses were registered with the American Quarter Horse Association (AQHA) and won hundreds of trophies throughout the southwest over a period of 40 years. Most mornings before going to work, he could be found at the barn, or riding one of the horses. I rode horses before I could ride a bicycle. In addition to the usual collection of dogs and cats, I also had a "pet" white-face Hereford bull named "Advanzidus". I have no idea where I came up with that name. It just popped out of my mouth one day when Mom asked me the bull's name. He weighed close to 2000 pounds but was as gentle as any dog we owned. He had a habit of laying crossways on the floor of the barn, blocking all passage until we could coax him into moving. I would sit on his massive body while he lay on the floor enjoying the attention. When we had visitors, Dad would show off the bull's passive disposition (and my courage) by having me sit on him while he stretched out on the floor. I was about 10 years old at the time. I also spent a lot of time competing at rodeos and horse show events. The walls of our living room were covered with trophies and award ribbons, mostly blue or red (first and second place). The trophies were prominently displayed on the fireplace mantle and tables throughout the house, attesting to my father's passion.

Though Dad loved all his animals, his favorite was "Brian H", a registered quarter horse stallion, whose bloodline included world-famous AQHA champion - "Ole Man". Brian H was acquired as a young colt at a local auction when Dad's ranch foreman traded a saddle for him. By the time "Brian H" retired from the show circuit, he had won every major event in the Southwest, and the International Quarter Horse Championship in Chicago in 1955. During his lifetime, he sired multiple champion off-springs. I often would tell my friends that I was named after "Brian H", rather than the reverse. He was infinitely more famous than I could ever dream of being, and I often said I thought Dad had a higher opinion of "Brian H" than of me.

(Original oil painting by nationally famous western artist Orren Mixer of A.Q.H.A Grand Champion stallion "Brian H", with namesake aboard. Several champion off springs are seen in the foreground; Bar B H Ranch in background.)

(Nationally famous western artist Orren Mixer)

(My father at his last ranch in Tioga, Texas, circa 1980)

I attended grades 1 through 12 at the Carrollton, but it came after a verbal confrontation between my father and the school superintendent of the Addison Elementary School district. Both schools competed for student enrollment much like today. Dad wanted me to have the best education possible, something he never had. So, when the Addison superintendent insisted that I was in its district, Dad rebelled. Addison Texas was a small town with a primitive education system. Carrollton, on the other hand, was higher rated scholastically, and offered interscholastic sports. Interestingly, our house straddled the line between Dallas County and Denton County. At that time the basis for settling disputes over school districts was "where the child slept". Addison and Carrollton were in Dallas County. My bedroom was on the north side of the house in Denton County where the only other school was in Hebron, a small village several miles north of our home, and had no interest in competing with Carrollton or Addison for my attendance. Therefore, Dad was allowed to choose the school I would attend. Addison had no say in the matter. Contest over. I enrolled at Carrollton Elementary in 1946.

2

CHAPTER

School Days

During my school years I was interested in sports. But at 5' 5" and 130 lbs. I was too small for football. Some of our linemen weighed over 200 lbs. So, I played basketball and baseball. At an early age I became interested in electronics, especially short-wave radio. I also became fascinated with airplanes and sailboats. When I was thirteen years old, I studied for my amateur radio license. At that time two exams were required. One was a written exam on electronic theory and the FCC rules, and a second exam on your ability to send and copy the Morse Code. The beginner exam was based on the theory and rules and a 5 word per minute Morse code exam. After the Novice exam I took an advanced exam on electronic theory and a 20 word per minute code test. Amateur Radio remains my favorite hobby to this day. More than 70 years later, I still communicate with people from all over the world on a small radio located in a closet.

My mother was born in Mineola Texas, a small town about 20 miles southeast of Dallas. Her childhood best friend was Louise Dantzler. In the early 1920s Louise's father had died when she was only a month old, so she and her mother moved to Long Beach, California. Being very pretty and talented, at the age of thirteen Louise entered a local beauty contest. One of the judges was actress Esther Ralston, who later played her mother in the original movie *Peter Pan,* ultimately becoming lifelong friends. When Louise didn't win the $25 first place prize, Ralston told the contest officials "you've got to give this little girl something." As a consolation prize, the judges gave Louise an interview with director Herbert Brenon for a role in *Peter Pan.* The studio had already screen tests of every ingénue in the business for the part of *Wendy.* But Brenon wanted an unknown, reasoning that it would be more like a fairy tale, and not right if the role was played by someone the audience knew or had been divorced. Louise Danzler, mother's best friend, was put under contract by the studio and given a new name - "Mary Brian". She and Mom stayed in touch throughout their remaining years. When I was born in 1939, I was named Brian in her honor. Mary Brian considered me her nephew, and I considered her my aunt for the rest of our lives.

Mary Brian was one of the Wampas Baby Stars in 1926, along with Mary Astor, Dolores Costello, Joan Crawford, Dolores del Río, Janet Gaynor, and Fay Wray. After successfully making the transition from silent movies to sound, she co-starred with Gary Cooper, Walter Huston and Richard Arlen in *The Virginian* (1929). In it she played a spirited frontier heroine and schoolmarm Molly Stark Wood, who was the love interest of *The Virginian* (Cooper). In 1936, she went to England and made three movies, including *The Amazing Quest of Ernest Bliss* starring opposite Cary Grant, with whom she became engaged for a short time. Over the course of 22 years, Mary Brian appeared in more than 79 movies. Like other older actresses, during the 1950s she had successful a career in television. Perhaps her most notable role was playing the title character's mother in *Meet Corliss Archer* in 1954. She also dedicated much of her time to portrait painting after retiring from acting and campaigned for the reelection of President Herbert Hoover in 1932. She married George Tomasini, an Academy Award nominated film editor. He had a decades long collaboration with movie director Alfred Hitchcock, editing nine of his movies between 1954 and 1964, including best-known works *Rear Window* (1954), *Vertigo* (1958), *North by Northwest* (1959), *Psycho* (1960), and *The Birds* (1963), as well as other popular films such as *Cape Fear* (1962). In 2012 a Motion Picture Editors Guild survey of the best edited films of all time listed four Hitchcock films edited by Tomasini. No other editor appeared on the list more than three times. The list included *Psycho*, *Vertigo*, *Rear Window*, and *North by Northwest*. Tomasini was nominated for an Academy Award for his film editing on *North by Northwest* but lost out to the film editor for *Ben Hur*.

(Mary Brian)

(George Tomasini)

3

CHAPTER

After High School

As previously mentioned, Dad's passion was his ranch, and particularly, his horses. And I naturally became part of that passion. At one time we had over 50 horses on the *Bar B H* ranch. Our registered cattle and horse brand was a bar followed by a "backwards B" attached to an "H" ... "–ꓭH".. Every year in October we attended the State Fair of Texas rodeo and horse show in Dallas. Dad always had 2 or 3 of our prize American Quarter Horse Association (AQHA) registered quarter horses entered in the various competitions. I participated in the "performance class" competition where the rider shows the horse's ability to turn left and right, while running at breakneck speed, coming to a full stop and laying down a perfect "11" in the arena dirt with his rear hoofs. The judges were certified by the AQHA. Each year during the rodeo, the producer would invite a guest celebrity that would ride around the arena waiving at the spectators in the stands from the back seat of a convertible. But in 1960 the guest of honor was James Garner, star of the new hit TV show "Maverick". The rodeo producer thought it would be a great idea for Garner to circle the arena on horseback. The rodeo producer confided to Dad that Garner was not an accomplished horseman as he often portrayed in the TV show, and they needed a gentle horse for Garner to ride. Dad told the show producer that he didn't have such a horse, but that I did. We had brought my personal horse, "Ginger", so I could ride in the grand entry at the beginning of each rodeo performance. Ginger was very gentle and easy to ride. It was arranged for Dad and me to meet with "Bret Maverick" in order for him to get acquainted with Ginger, "the wonder horse" (at least in my mind). One of Ginger's tricks was to bow her head when the National Anthem was played at the rodeo's opening ceremonies. When I showed Garner how it was done, he was amazed. Each night the crowd would cheer when Garner, leading the opening Grand Entry ceremony, dropped the reins on Ginger's neck, her cue to reverently bow during the playing of the National Anthem. Bret Maverick and "Ginger, the wonder horse", were the stars at the Texas State Fair Rodeo.

For the entire week, I showed Garner the sights and exhibits at the State Fair. After the rodeo and horse show, Garner returned to Hollywood, and I returned to work at the trucking company. As we were saying goodbye, Garner invited me to visit him in Hollywood. A short time later, Dad received an 8x10 studio photograph of "Bret Maverick" from Garner. At the bottom, he had inscribed – ***"To the Hunsakers – Your Texas hospitality is even bigger than the State. Thank you again. Jim Garner"***. About a year later I flew to California and met with Garner at the Warner Brothers studios where he was making the movie "The Children's Hour", co-starring Audrey Hepburn and Shirley McClain. I was shown around the studios and introduced to Jack Warner, the president of Warner Brothers, as well as several other actors. My biggest thrill came when Garner took me to the studio next door, where Elvis Presley was making the movie "Blue Hawaii". During a break in the filming, Garner introduced me to Elvis. Very congenial and shaking my hand, he asked about my life back in Texas. To this day I have fond memories of that close up and personal meeting with the "King of Rock and Roll".

(The "Maverick" studio portrait autographed by actor James Garner)

4

CHAPTER

John Selmon, The SMS Ranch, and The Texas Cowboy Reunion

John Selmon was born in the late 1880s, in Stamford, Texas (near Abilene). Throughout his entire life he worked on the Swenson SMS ranch, starting out as a ranch hand at age 14, and eventually becoming the ranch foreman for the last 50 years of his life. He and his wife, Emma, had one son, Tony, who went to the University of Texas, and became a doctor, opening a practice in Stamford, until his passing several years ago. John's uncle, also named John Selmon, was a deputy sheriff in El Paso, Texas for many years. He is credited with killing the famous outlaw, John Wesley Hardin, in a gunfight in El Paso in the late 1880s. This was verified from true historic reports and newspaper accounts of the gunfight.

Each year, during the 4th of July week, the Stamford Fairgrounds Committee put on a weeklong rodeo and horse show, referred to as "The Texas Cowboy Reunion". This was during the late 1950s and 60s, when my father would load up an 18-wheel horse van, and other vehicles with horses and camping supplies, and we would go to the Fairgrounds and camp out for a week while the rodeo and horse show was in progress. This continued for several years while I was in high school and after graduating. Our campground was the favorite place to hang out during rodeo week. We frequently had most of the rodeo cowboys and horse people stopping by for breakfast, which was cooked over an open fire by a friend of Dad's. In the evening, there was always a cold beer at happy hour. John Selmon was the center of attention at this time, having already become a legend in the real cowboy world. He would sit around the campfire in the evenings telling his stories, all of which were hard to believe, but in fact were true. He was a modern-day Will Rogers, with a similar philosophy about life. We would sit and listen to him until the wee hours of the morning … sometimes all night. When dawn came, John would drink the last of his beer, hop on his horse or in his ranch truck, and head back to the rodeo grounds to pick up where he had left off the day before. John Selmon was definite "one of a kind". There are none like him left any more. During his ranching career, he had lost parts of 3 fingers on one hand, and 1 on the other hand from getting them entangled in a rope, or accidentally cutoff by a saw, or ax. He smoked unfiltered Herbert Tareyton, or Camel cigarettes, and would put the ashes in the turned-up cuffs of his jeans – even when we were sitting on bare ground at the camp by the campfire!

A funny incident occurred one year during the rodeo, when John and his older brother from New Mexico, Hoot Selmon, were returning to our camp from the rodeo grounds late one evening. They showed up with blood on their faces, and torn clothing. Upon being asked what happened, he told my father that he and Hoot had been jumped by 3 young black men trying to rob them. John and Hoot had a habit of carrying long hickory canes used for prodding the cattle through the chutes at the fairgrounds and holding pens. The 3 blacks made the fatal mistake of underestimating these two "old cowboys". The fight was short and sweet. After it was over, all 3 black men were carted off in an ambulance to the local hospital with an assortment of broken bones, serious cuts and concussions. John and Hoot only received superficial cuts and abrasions, which only required some cleaning with and a couple of "Band Aids". They were in their 70s when this incident happened. The 3 black men were in their 20s.

On another occasion, during roundup one year, John and his hands were herding cattle from a large pasture into a "holding pen" at the rail head for shipment to market. Mr. Swenson, owner of the Swenson ranch, and who lived in New York, had come to Stamford to witness the roundup. After the last cow had passed through the entrance gate to the holding pen, Swenson asked John what the "headcount" was, i.e. how many were to be loaded on the freight cars. John replied, "Well, Mr. Swenson, I reckon there are 106 head." Swenson exploded and replied, "John, you can't "reckon"!! We must know exactly how many cattle there are in the pen! Now take them back out and run them through again! And this time we will count them one at a time, together!" Following Swenson's orders, John had the cattle removed from the holding pen into a larger area, and proceeded to run them through the gate again one at a time, as he had been instructed by Swenson. When the last cow had entered the holding pen Swenson asked John how many he counted. John replied, "106". With an embarrassed look on his face, Swenson agreed with the count, whereupon John, replied, "Well, Mr. Swenson, I reckon I reckoned right." John Selmon died in 1984 at the age of 86, still working a full day on the SMS ranch, having never lived anywhere else.

5

Off To College

During my senior year of high school, I had been looking at colleges offering courses in electronics. All of the schools in the Dallas-Ft. Worth area offered only degrees in business or education. The closest college offering studies in electronics was in Houston. Rice Institute (as it was called then) had an electronics engineering program. Though my father was generous, he was very protective of the family, which came from having to drop out of school to help support his mother and three siblings. Dad agreed for me to take flying lessons, but "suggested" that I apply for admission to Southern Methodist University in Dallas. Years later, being able to fly an airplane became more than just a hobby. It became a means of survival, as the reader will later learn. A year after graduating from Carrollton, I married my high school sweetheart and enrolled at Southern Methodist University in Dallas. One year later, Kevin, our first child, was born. Two years later, we welcomed our second son, Kerry. From experience, I recommend never starting a family while preparing for college! Following two years of juggling parent responsibilities and school, I dropped out of SMU and returned to work at the family company. However, there were two notable experiences from my time at SMU. One, I had a class and became friends with "Dandy" Don Meridith, starting quarterback on the SMU Mustangs football team, and the original Dallas Cowboys. Secondly, I made the SMU swim team as the only "walk-on". In 1959, our freshman team won the Southwest Conference 400-meter freestyle relay event.

One morning at the office over coffee, me and Bobby, the company pilot were having an intense discussion about something. Finally realizing he wasn't winning the argument, he jokingly said, "You should be a lawyer!" The idea stuck in the back of my mind. Shortly thereafter, I decide to finish college and enroll in a law school. Commuting daily from my home to North Texas State University in Denton, Texas, I graduated in 1965 with a degree in business administration. During my final year at NTSU I was accepted for admission to Baylor Law School in Waco, 90 miles south of Dallas. This pleased my parents and was easy for family visits. I might point out, Baylor Law school is based on the "quarter system", rather than the more widely used "semester system". A school year at Baylor was four 3-month sessions, as opposed to 2 four and a half month semesters per year at other schools. By taking a 14-hour course load each quarter, I was able to graduate in 27 months, compared to the normal three-year term at other schools. However, I don't recommend it. It was a grind not having any time off between the sessions, but I wanted to make up for the lost years spent at SMU. I was almost 27 years old, with a wife and 2 children. Most of my classmates were in their early 20s, with no families. After graduating from Baylor, I passed the Texas Bar exam in the fall of 1967. I had finally finished college, had a law degree and license to practice law.

One interesting event occurred while in Waco. We lived in a large apartment complex on the south side of town. Kerry was about 4 or 5 years old at the time and would get up earlier than the rest of the family on Saturday mornings to watch cartoons. One morning I came in the living room and Kerry told me he saw the police chasing and shooting at a car. I first thought he was talking about a cartoon he had been watching. But he insisted he had seen it happened outside our apartment. When I questioned him about what he saw he said, "I was standing outside by the parking lot and this car came driving by real fast with the police chasing and shooting at him." Naturally I was surprised but dismissed it as wild imagination. However, a few minutes later the local news announced there had been a police chase involving an escaped prisoner from the McLennan County jail. I immediately called the police and told them what my son had told me. They verified that there was an escaped prisoner and the police had located him at our apartment complex and that a high-speed chase and shooting had occurred. The officer took my name and address, and a few minutes later an officer arrived and spoke with Kerry about what he saw. The escapee had eluded the police for the moment, but we learned later he had been recaptured and returned to jail. The man had been arrested by the Waco police for burglary and car theft in another town. From no more than 10 feet away, Kerry had witnessed a real live "shoot-out", complete with speeding cars and real bullets, just like he watched every morning on TV. Quite exciting for a 5-year-old, but scary for Mom and Dad. Eventually, both of my sons finished college. Kerry has two grown children, Melissa and Scott. Melissa is a professional dance instructor with her own studio and Scott is married and works as a production manager for a nationally known manufacturing company. He and his wife have two young children, making Kerry a grandfather and me and his mother great grandparents. Kevin, however, has remained a bachelor, and has toured most of the free countries in world.

6

CHAPTER

Celebrities and Professional Athletes

During the summer of 1960, the National Football League expanded into select cities and Dallas, Texas was one of the new markets the league was interested in. Local Dallas oilman and developer, Clint Murchison, was granted an NFL franchise for a new team to be known as the Dallas Cowboys. At the same time, the new "upstart" American Football League was being organized by another Dallas oilman, Lamar Hunt. Dad was friends with both Murchison and Hunt from his earlier oil field trucking days. Hunt's team was called the "Dallas Texans", and he contacted Dad asking for a favor. His players needed summer jobs. AFL player's salaries in 1960 were a far cry from today's multimillion dollar contracts. Most of the players were fresh out of college with families and needed a second job to survive. Professional football players in 1960 were paid by the game, meaning – "no play, no pay". Back then, playing football in the AFL was a part-time job. Dad agreed to hire Max Boydston, an All-American tight end from Oklahoma. Boydston worked at the company as a salesman during the week and was a starting offensive end for the Texans on weekends. Boydston and I became good friends. Max and some of his fellow Texan teammates formed a summer barnstorming basketball team, traveling around the state playing exhibition games with the local high school teams. Being a personal friend, I was invited to join their group. I was the only "non-professional" athlete member of the team.

Because of Dad's friendship with Hunt and the part-time employment of Boydston, we were given sideline passes to the Dallas Texans home games. Over the course of the next few years, I made friends with other players, as well as head coach Hank Stram. After three years of competing with the Dallas

Cowboys for spectator attendance, it was obvious the Dallas professional football market would not support two local teams. One team had to relocate. So, in 1963, probably after losing a coin toss, Hunt moved his team to Kansas City, Missouri, renaming them the "Kansas City Chiefs" and ultimately winning five Super Bowl championships, as of this writing.

(Max Boydston – NCAA All American at Oklahoma, and AFL All Pro with the Kansas City Chiefs)

Another chance meeting and friendship with a celebrity happened while attending a PGA golf tournament in Dallas. World famous PGA professional Gary Player was at the Byron Nelson Invitational Tournament at Preston Trails Country Club, not far from our home. During an interview with a local newspaper reporter, Player had mentioned that he was in Texas not just to play golf, but he also wanted to find some good quarter horse stock for his ranch in South Africa. At the conclusion of his round, I approached Player at the clubhouse and introduced myself. I told him about Dad's collection of registered quarter horses. To my surprise, Player said he would love to meet my father, and look at our horses. After he showered and change clothes, we drove to the ranch. Player liked what he saw and bought three young horses. Dad threw in a fourth one for free and arranged to have them shipped to Player's ranch in South Africa. Thereafter, each year when Player returned to Dallas for the Nelson tournament, he would stop by our home for a visit and often stay for supper. He also invited us to visit his home in Pretoria, South Africa, but unfortunately, we could never arrange the trip.

(My friend, Gary Player)

7

CHAPTER

Assistant District Attorney

After graduating from law school, I returned to Dallas and was employed by Henry Wade, the long-time Dallas DA, as an assistant district attorney. Wade had gained notoriety prosecuting famous cases during his many years in office. However, none were as famous as the capital murder trial of Jack Ruby, the Dallas nightclub owner who shot Lee Harvey Oswald, the accused assassin of President John F. Kennedy in 1963. After being captured and interrogated by Dallas Police Captain Will Fritz, another family friend, Oswald was escorted to the underground parking lot of the Dallas Police Department to be transported to the county jail 10 blocks away. Without warning, Ruby stepped out of the crowd and pulled a small pistol from under his coat and shot Oswald at point blank range, a historic turn of events witnessed by the spectators and millions on national television.

District Attorney Wade had suggested to me that I should join the Federal Bureau of Investigation (FBI) for a year before coming to the DA's office in order to gain experience in criminal investigation techniques. The FBI, CIA, and several other government agencies, as well as private firms, had visited Baylor Law School on recruiting trips during my senior year. But I was anxious to get into the courtroom and did not accept the FBI job offer – a decision I regretted ever since. So, upon graduation, I returned to Dallas and became an Assistant District Attorney. This was November 1967, after having passed the Texas State Bar exam in October. My time spent in the Dallas DA's office can be best characterized as "post graduate law school". After being sworn in by a Dallas District Judge, I was assigned to one of the county courts prosecuting misdemeanors (petty theft, DWI and shoplifting). A few months later, I was transferred to a district court where I prosecuted major crimes (felonies) such as murder, burglary, and robbery.

In 1970 I joined a local Masonic Lodge. My father and uncle both were Masons. One of the strict rules of the Order is that a father, or another relative cannot invite you to join the Masonic Order. Dad was very happy when I told him I wanted to become a Mason. Another rule about the Masons is that nothing may be communicated in writing. Everything must be by "mouth to ear" from one Mason to another, or to a candidate preparing for initiation. In order to learn the lessons required for initiation, a candidate working with a private instructor must memorize certain ritual passages taken mostly from the Bible. Fortunately for me, one of the DA investigators was a certified Masonic instructor. Working with him after office hours for several weeks, I passed the first three Masonic degrees and was initiated into the Masonic Order as a Master Mason of Masonic Lodge #201 in Lewisville, Texas, one of the oldest Masonic lodges in the State.

After Master Mason, the next level is degrees 4 through 32. This initiation, unlike the first three, does not involve memorization. Rather, the candidate watches live enactments highlighting the principles and life lessons of Masonry. These "plays" are performed by lodge members from around the county. The program starts early in the morning and runs to late evening. After completing the degrees 4 through the 32, we were given the opportunity to join a final Masonic group called "The Shriners", the social group in the Masonic Order. The Shriners initiation is not secretive like the previous rituals, although the candidate must be a 32nd degree Mason before he is eligible to join the Shriners. I explain this because it is my personal connection with Ted Hinton. I was initiated into the Scottish Rite Shrine in 1970. During the initiation ritual the candidate must "walk the hot sands", as it is referred to. It is a reference to a passage from the Bible wherein prophets crossed the "hot sands" of the Egyptian desert. The candidate is escorted across a "staged" hot sands during his initiation by his sponsor. Ted Hinton was my sponsor and guide during my induction into the Shriners. More on Ted Hinton and our personal friendship appears later in the book

8

CHAPTER

Close Call for A "Texas Ranger"

A memorable incident occurred while I was in the DA's office. It involved two men who had escaped from the Dallas County jail while being transported from one facility to another, resulting in a shootout after they were located by sheriff officers in an area known as the "Trinity River Bottom", a dry riverbed on the southwest outskirts of the city. The two police officers had been killed trying to apprehend the fugitives. A massive city-wide manhunt was quickly organized with several law enforcement agencies involved. The Dallas Police Department received an anonymous tip that one of the men was hiding in a garage apartment next to a small frame house in East Dallas. Earlier, I had become active in Masonic initiations with my local lodge, and as a "special member" of the Dallas Sheriff's Office Ritual Team. The Sheriff's ritual team had a reputation as being one of the best ritual teams in the county. As the only "non-deputy" member, and an assistant DA, I was close friends with sheriff Clarence Jones and other law enforcement officials. I was frequently called upon for legal advice involving search and arrest warrants. When the Sheriff's office received information concerning the location of one of the escaped fugitives, a raid on the garage apartment was quickly organized, involving the multiple agencies. I was asked to go along as an official observer during the raid. The police wanted to be sure there were no legal issues during the execution of the search warrant and arrest of the fugitive. Therefore, I was included in the planning and details of how the raid would be carried out and present during the raid and apprehension. Shortly before daybreak, we arrived at the location and I was stationed at a position behind the front line of officers, crouched behind a large bush out of the line of fire. It should be noted here that I was dressed in a dark suit, white shirt and tie, Stetson hat, and boots. I could have easily been confused as a Texas Ranger. A mistake which almost got me shot I learned a few days later.

The lead officers approached the door to the apartment and knocked. No response. A door ram was employed, and the officers rushed the apartment yelling **"POLICE! HANDS UP!** This was a single room apartment occupied by a man and woman asleep in bed at the time. Startled by the intrusion, the man reached for his bedside lamp. This action resulted in the lead officer firing his weapon, hitting the man in the shoulder. After clearing the room, the occupants were removed, and the wounded man was placed in an ambulance waiting on the street in the event of injuries. Once the police had a good look at the man, they realized he was not the fugitive. A mistake had been made with the house number when it was given to the police by the informant. Upon realizing their mistake, the raiding party regrouped and initiated the raid on the house next door where I was crouched behind the bush. My back was facing the room in the house where the fugitive was actually hiding with his girlfriend, only a few feet away. Days later, one of the officers who had participated in the raid came to my office and informed me how close I had come to being shot. Apparently, the fugitive was watching the initial raid at the wrong apartment and thinking he would ultimately be discovered, told his girlfriend that before he was captured, he was going to "take out that Texas Ranger" ... apparently meaning me! His girlfriend convinced him not to shoot but to remain hidden and hopefully the raiding party would leave. Luckily, the raid continued, and the fugitive was apprehended without gunfire, and a "Texas Ranger" wasn't shot. I never went on another raid and made sure I dressed like your everyday car salesman when I was out in public.

After a couple of years as an assistant DA, two of my fellow assistant DAs and I decided to leave the DA's office and form a private law firm in an office across the street from the Dallas County courthouse. A year later my cousin joined the firm as a partner. We were now representing the same class of people we had been putting in jail for the past couple of years. But the bills had to be paid, and we no longer had the luxury of a regular paycheck. So, we accepted any case that walked through our door – misdemeanors, felonies, divorces, child custody, contracts, and even a few bankruptcies.

9

CHAPTER

The Ambush of Clyde Barrow and Bonnie Parker

"Bonnie was a waitress in a small cafe.
Clyde Barrow was a rounder who took her away.
They both robbed and killed until both of them died.
So goes the legend of Bonnie and Clyde."
(Opening verse from the Merle Haggard album, "Ballad of Bonnie and Clyde")

Probably one of the most interesting people I knew was Ted Hinton previously mentioned in Chapter 6 during my Shriner initiation. When I knew him, he had retired from law enforcement, and was living a private life as a motel owner in Irving, Texas. He and Dad had become friends several years earlier when Hinton was a deputy sheriff in Dallas, and later when he owned a small trucking company. Ted nicknamed me "Cotton", because in those days I had very bright, blonde hair. He would frequently come by Dad's office, and we would go to lunch. Each time he would enter the receptionist area, and greet everyone with a loud but polite, "Good morning!". Then he would ask, "Where's the big cheese?", referring to my father. The entire office staff would have a big laugh.

However, history will best remember Ted Hinton as being in the posse that ambushed and killed Clyde Barrow and Bonnie Parker, the famous 1930s duo that robbed banks, and killing 12 people during their short-lived (2 years) criminal career. Ted and Grace Hinton had a son, Linton "Boots" Hinton. Boots was a couple of years older than me, but close enough that we shared common interests as adolescents - mainly baseball. I recall the time we were invited to have dinner at the Hinton home in

Irving, Texas. After refreshments and dinner, the topic of conversation turned to "Bonnie & Clyde", the notorious outlaws from west Dallas, and the well-documented ambush led by Ted Hinton and his fellow law enforcement officers. Ted brought out a large photo album of black and white original photos. Graphic pictures of the bullet-riddled bodies of Clyde Barrow and Bonnie Parker in the morgue, and the bullet-riddled 1932 Ford Sedan at the ambush scene at the Texas/ Louisiana border. The ambush spot was on a remote, tree-lined county road just across the state line, near Gibsland and Arcadia. The posse consisted of Ted Hinton and Bob Alcorn, both Dallas Deputy Sheriffs, who had been assigned by Dallas County Sheriff Lester "Smoot" Smid, specifically to track down Barrow and Parker. Assisting Hinton and Alcorn was former Texas Ranger Frank Hamer, and Manny Gault, on loan from Texas Prison Director Lee Simmons. Also in the group was Arcadia County Sheriff Henderson Jordan, and Deputy Prentis Oakley. The plan was to have several two member teams positioned along the south side of the road, spaced a few yards apart. Hinton and Alcorn were in the first, most easterly position. Barrow was rumored to be coming from gang member Henry Methvin's father home in Arcadia. Hinton and Alcorn would therefore have the first opportunity to confront Barrow and Parker. If they were coming from Texas toward Arcadia (to Methvin's house), Frank Hamer in position #6, furthest west, would have first crack at the duo. As it turned out, Barrow was driving from Arcadia back to Texas. Deputy Sheriffs Ted Hinton and Bob Alcorn would be the first to confront the killers.

As the ambush team was getting ready, Irvin Methvin, gang member Henry Methvin's father, showed up and confronted Hinton about the "trap" they were setting for his son. Methvin was asked to turn around and go back to Arcadia. When he refused, Alcorn handcuffed him to a tree, and moved his Model A Ford truck to the opposite side of the road, jacked up with one tire removed. This proved to be a very strategic move, as it turned out, because as the killers approached the area where Hinton and his team were waiting, Barrow slowed to a stop after seeing Methvin's truck in the road up on jacks. At that moment, Hinton yelled, "HALT!" and immediately started firing his Browning automatic rifle. After expending all 21 rounds into the car, he picked up his high-powered shotgun and continued until it was empty, not giving Barrow and Parker any advance warning, which had proven to be a big mistake by previous police, resulting in them being outgunned by the killers. The Barrow gang killing spree ended at 9:15 on the morning of May 23, 1934.

In describing the shoot-out scene, Ted told us that Clyde and Bonnie had made it known they would never be taken alive. They had killed 12 people, several of them police officers, and they had escaped capture several times by now. Clyde Barrow knew that if he was captured the electric chair in Huntsville would be his fate. They felt Bonnie Parker would spend some time in prison, but would eventually be released, and without Clyde as an influence, could return to a normal life. She never got that chance. The team of officers had earlier decided that because of their history of shooting first when confronted by the police, they would not give them the opportunity to surrender. It was too risky and would likely result in more officers being killed or seriously wounded. Therefore, the plan was to remain hidden behind the trees and bushes at the roadside, and when Clyde's car was within range, with high power automatic rifles and shotguns, the posse would immediately open fire from both sides. The rest is history. After two years, and twelve murders, on May 23, 1934, Clyde Barrow and Bonnie Parker had finally met their ultimate fate, thanks to the dogged determination and police work of Ted Hinton, and his courageous team members. The "Bonnie and Clyde" era had finally and thankfully come to an end.

Several years later, Hollywood made a popular movie about the life and times of Clyde Barrow and Bonnie Parker, entitled "Bonnie and Clyde". It starred Warren Beatty as Clyde Barrow, and Faye Dunaway as Bonnie Parker. Ted Hinton was hired as "special advisor" to the director, and his name appears in the credits of the movie. It had been agreed by the members of the posse that their story would finally be told by the last surviving member of the posse, which was ultimately, Ted Hinton. Hinton passed away on October 27, 1977, being the last surviving member of the posse that had successfully hunted down and killed Clyde Barrow and Bonnie Parker. Ted Hinton wrote a book entitled "AMBUSH". It remains the only authentic story of the lives, and accurate account of the deaths, of Clyde Barrow and Bonnie Parker. It can be found in most bookstores, or online at Amazon. Many of the events related here by the author were taken from and verified from Ted Hinton's book.

(The ambush team. Ted Hinton, top left)

(Over 150 bullets riddled Clyde & Bonnie's 1932 Model A Ford sedan)

(Ted Hinton's Colt 380 carried on the Bonnie & Clyde ambush. It was given to my father. Currently owned by the author.)

Fast forward to my law practice days in Dallas. A local car dealer and friend, whom Dad had purchased automobiles from over the years, W. O. Bankston, was acquainted with a member of the Barrow family. Clyde's youngest sister, Marie, was married to man who had been released from prison after serving time for burglary, and they had purchased a small frame house in East Dallas. Having been convicted previously, he knew the next conviction would be as a habitual offender (3 times or more), resulting in a life sentence.

Marie's husband had been arrested and charged with possession of marijuana shortly after moving into the small frame house. Barrow's sister and her husband were referred to me by Bankston for representation. Their story was that although her husband was an ex-con, and a long-time burglar, he had never been involved in drugs. Bankston told me that he knew her, and her husband well enough to know they were telling the truth. He was likely being harassed because of his relation to the infamous Barrow family. Their explanation was that shortly after purchasing the house, a couple of young Hispanic boys knocked on their door and ask if they could trim some trees in the back yard, near the alley. Apparently, a couple of them had grown over the fence, and were hanging out in the alley. The two young boys offered to do the trimming for a nominal amount, and it was agreed for them to trim the trees. The boys trimmed the trees and left, only to be arrested a short time later by the local police. It seems the tree trimmings were actually from an over-grown marijuana plant. Under pressure and questioning by the police, they said they had "bought" the marijuana from Marie's husband. A complete lie, but good enough for the police to arrest him, after learning that he was the husband of Clyde Barrow's sister.

After being hired, I requested that we be allowed to present testimony to the Dallas County Grand Jury, and have the accused husband tell the grand jury his version of what happened. By introducing the dated sales contract on the house, we proved unquestionably the house had been purchased and subsequently occupied only a few days before the "tree trimmers" were caught with the marijuana. And since the marijuana plants were very tall, it was obvious the marijuana had been there long before Marie Barrow and her husband arrived. They both testified they had no idea what marijuana even looked like. "I'm a burglar, not a dope dealer", Marie Barrow's husband told the grand jury. The Grand Jury took less than 30 minutes to "No Bill" (acquit) Marie Barrow's husband. During the next 5 years, the law firm represented an unusual assortment of people with a variety of legal problems. Most were average, run-of-the-mill legal matters. However, one client stands out above all the rest due to his notoriety and reputation.

10

Texas Pardons a Famous Gambler

Lester Ben "Benny" Binion was a product of his time and place. He was born in 1904 in Pilot Grove, Texas, had a bad second-grade education, and could barely read or write. He spent his formative years traveling with horse traders and gamblers. Benny liked to say, "Tough times make tough people." He is best known as the founder and owner of the world-renowned Las Vegas casino, "Binion's Horseshoe Casino", which was located in the middle of downtown Las Vegas, Nevada. He had "relocated" to Las Vegas in 1953, after being released from Federal prison for failure to pay income tax. The reason I say "re-located" is because at the time he was charged for the non-payment of income tax, he was operating an illegal dice game at a downtown Dallas hotel. The State of Texas also had a warrant for his arrest for "keeping an illegal gaming operation", a state offense which resulted in a 4-year sentence. The Federal charge carried a 5-year sentence.

Dallas County Sheriff, Bill Decker, and Binion were friends, as often was the case in those days. So, at the time of his arrest in Dallas, an agreement was reached between the Feds and Dallas County that Binion would serve his federal sentence for non-payment of taxes, and then be given credit on his state charges of keeping a gaming operation. So Binion voluntarily surrendered to the Feds and was handed over to the United States Marshal for transport to Leavenworth, Kansas to begin his 5-year federal prison term.

But something unusual happened between the time Binion was placed in Leavenworth and his release almost 5 years later. The Texas authorities had never withdrawn the arrest warrant for Binion's gambling offense in Dallas. Several attempts were made to correct the problem, all to no avail. However, the Federal prison officials failed to check the status of the Texas charges and released Binion from federal prison in 1953. Being the ultimate survivor, Binion headed straight for Las Vegas, Nevada, a town noted for its "friendly hospitality", to begin his new life as a successful casino owner, while Dallas County Sheriff Decker kept the Texas warrant locked away in a desk drawer, there to be forgotten for almost 20 years.

Benny Binion opened Binion's Horseshoe Casino in 1957, which later became famous for attracting high stakes poker players from around the world to his annual "World Series of Poker". The "buy-in" was $10,000. An unheard-of entry fee for a poker tournament at the time. But Binion was a visionary. The game was "no-limit", and it attracted the world's top professional gamblers of the day. The ultimate champion was the last man standing, i.e., the rest of the field had lost their entire bank. It is still the premier poker tournament in the world today. The buy-in today is $100,000, a tribute Benny Binion's incredible vision, and foresight. It's no wonder he is probably the most successful and well-known professional gambler that ever lived.

At a chance meeting at a horse show in west Texas, my father and Binion ran into each other. Dad, surprised to see his old friend, asked Benny why he was chancing arrest by showing up in Texas, where there was still an active arrest warrant for him. Binion explained that he was visiting his daughter and son-in-law and their children in Amarillo and wanted to see the horse show. During the discussion, Binion mentioned that he wished there was some way he could get the warrant withdrawn and credit for his time served in federal prison. He told my father that he had employed 8 or 10 attorneys over the years to look into the matter, but none were successful. Dad mentioned that I had graduated from law school and had been in the Dallas District Attorney's office for the past 2 years and had opened my own law office. Dad told Binion I might be interested in looking into his legal problems. Binion ask Dad to have me call him. Shortly after Dad's return from the horse show, he filled me in on his conversation with Binion. I made the call to Las Vegas and spoke with Binion. I told him I had done some research on the various ways to obtain a termination of a criminal sentence and thought I might have an idea. He invited me to fly out to Vegas to discuss my idea.

The normal procedure for eliminating a prison sentence is a pardon by the Governor. However, this method requires getting a letter from the Texas Board of Pardons & Paroles stating they have no objection to the granting of a pardon that basically erases the conviction. At this time, Jack Ross, the current chairman of the Texas Board of Pardons & Paroles, was not inclined to write such a letter. He had been approached over the years by most of Binion's previous lawyers, offering money (i.e.- bribes) in return for the pardon letter. Ross was a staunch law and order guy and was very much offended by the bribery attempts by the various Binion attorneys. To say the least, he had a bad taste in his mouth when it came to the subject of Benny Binion in general. My job in obtaining a full settlement of Benny Binion's criminal sentence was further compounded by the improper attempts to influence a government official. I had to approach Jack Ross, and the Texas Board of Pardons & Paroles completely different – a fresh approach, and one that distanced me from the previous attorneys.

During my research on pardons and paroles, I found an option that was a "compromise" but would still result in terminating the Texas warrant. One that the Pardon & Parole Board chairman might accept. And more importantly, it would allow the chairman to save face, and not compromise his principles. This alternative is called a "Commutation of Sentence". This procedure isn't the same as the granting of a full pardon where the crime is forgiven and ceases to exist on record. A Commutation of Sentence instead changes the term of the sentence by reducing it to time served. The person still has a conviction on his record but is released from any further requirement of serving time in a prison. However, a commutation still requires the approval (or at least no objection) by 3 local law enforcement officials, namely - (1) the judge of the court where the original sentence was imposed, (2) the sheriff of the county where the offense occurred, and (3) the District Attorney who prosecuted the individual. In Binion's case, it was Henry Wade, Dallas County District Attorney, my former employer.

The first two letters were easily obtained. The presiding judge of the Dallas court that sentenced Binion had passed away a few years earlier. The law states that when this is the case, the current judge of the sentencing court may write the "no objection" letter. In our case, the current judge was fair minded, and personally enjoyed gambling excursions to Las Vegas. Besides, writing a letter stating that he had no objection to Binion's commutation of sentence didn't reflect on him personally, since he really wasn't the judge who sentenced Binion in 1953. The second letter I needed was from the Dallas County Sheriff. Again, as in the case of the sentencing court judge, previous sheriff Decker had since passed away, and a member of the Dallas County Sheriff's Masonic Ritual Team. Plus, as I previously related, I had a close relationship with the Sheriff's office when I was an assistant DA. However, the last letter wouldn't be as easy as the first two. Dallas District Attorney Henry Wade had prosecuted Binion on the gambling charges and was reluctant to write a letter to the Texas Board of Pardons & Paroles approving the commutation. Wade said it would be admitting that he had made a mistake prosecuting Binion. Finally at my suggestion, he agreed to write a letter stating he would not "oppose" a commutation of sentence for Binion. I wasn't certain Wade's letter would be enough to satisfy the Parole Board, but fortunately the Parole Board accepted it.

With the three letters in hand, I filed an application for the commutation of sentence for Binion with the Texas Board of Pardons & Paroles. Surprisingly, in short order I received a letter from Jack Ross, the chairman of the Texas Board of Pardons & Paroles which read: "Upon further investigation and review, the request for the Commutation of Sentence for Applicant, Lester Ben Binion had been unanimously approved by the board, and that no further action was required". The Texas warrant was ordered withdrawn, and Benny Binion was finally, and officially declared a free man. I immediately called Binion and told him the good news. Excited, he told me to get on the first plane to Vegas where he and friends would be waiting at the casino for a long overdue celebration.

However, there was one last thing to do before heading to Las Vegas. I had to get the official "Commutation of Sentence" signed by the Texas Governor. Although my father and Governor Smith were personal friends and we had supported Smith's election campaign, and I can't say this didn't have some effect on my efforts, in reality once the Board of Pardons & Paroles recommends a commutation or parole, it is a routine for the Governor to approve and preparation of the official document. The Governor's office notified me a couple of days later they had received the commutation recommendation from the Parole Board and that the official document would be mailed, or I could pick it up in person at the Governor's office. Well, this was a "no-brainer". The next day I was on a flight to Austin to visit the Governor of Texas. The following day I was on a flight from Dallas to Las Vegas.

When I arrived at Binion's Horseshoe, the reservation clerk handed me a room key, and said I was already checked in, and that Mr. Binion was waiting for me in the restaurant. Apparently, the news of my arrival was already widespread. At a large round table in the rear of the restaurant sat 4 or 5 gentlemen, and Benny Binion. Benny waived me over to the table and introduced me to his friends. Their names have since faded from my memory, but their reputations in the community hasn't. Among the group was a Nevada state representative, a local judge, and the sheriff of McCarran County. With a big smile, Binion shook my hand and said, "Let's see it". I handed him a large envelope containing the official Commutation of Sentence, complete with a large gold seal and signed - **"Preston Smith, Governor of the State of Texas"**. Benny choked up and gave me a hug. Whereupon the others at the table stood and applauded. This experience remains the single biggest moment of my entire legal career, with the possible exception of the day I learned that I had passed the Texas Bar.

From the time I met with Binion in Las Vegas and the obtaining the commutation, Binion and I had never discussed a fee. First of all, I was very excited to be representing such a famous person and was focused on succeeding where other lawyers had failed. Looking back, I don't think the subject of a fee ever crossed my mind. But true to his character, Binion said he would meet me in my room in a few minutes. I was waiting when he walked into the room and thanked me for what I had done. Then he tossed an envelope on the bed and said, "I'll see you downstairs and we'll have a drink to celebrate" (although he never drank), and then he walked out. I opened the envelope and almost fainted. Inside was a hundred crisp $100 bills in bank wrappers and a gold watch crafted inside a $10 gold coin with a genuine alligator band. The watch was later appraised at $10,000.

I spent the next few days meeting several friends of Binion's and enjoying the moment as a special guest of the famous casino owner. One of the regulars at the Horseshoe was Hollywood character actor, Chill Wills. Being a fellow Texan, we immediately hit it off, and spent the next few days laughing and listening to his wild stories. For sure, there was never a dull moment with Chill Wills around. This was in 1970. A short time later Dad and I were invited to Binion's Montana ranch for a quail hunt. All of his Montana rancher friends were there and wanted to shake my hand. Obviously, I was overwhelmed by the "celebrity status" I experienced that week.

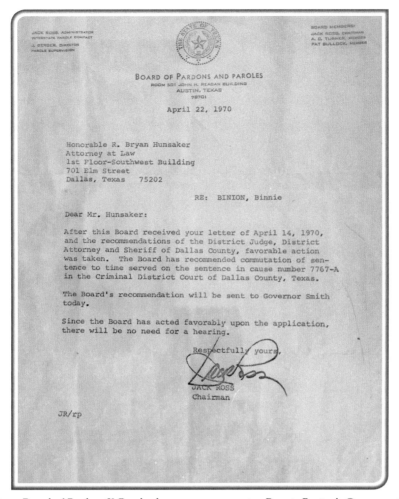

(Texas Board of Pardon & Paroles letter to me approving Bennie Benion's Commutation of Sentence, dated and signed by Chairman Jack Ross, April 22, 1970)

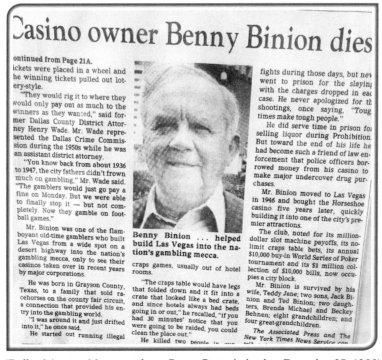

(Dallas Morning News article on Benny Binion's death – December 27, 1989)

Another "celebrity" client was Jerry Lee Lewis, the Cajun singer, song writer and piano player. Nicknamed "The Killer", he was described as "rock 'n' roll's first great wild man". A pioneer of rock 'n' roll and rockabilly music, he made his early recordings in 1956 at Sun Records in Memphis, Tennessee. "Crazy Arms" sold 300,000 copies in the Southern United States, but it was his 1957 hit "Whole Lotta Shakin' Goin' On" that shot Lewis to worldwide fame. He followed this with the major hits "Great Balls of Fire". Lewis was the last surviving member of Sun Records' Million Dollar Quartet and the album *Class of '55*, which also included Johnny Cash, Carl Perkins, Roy Orbison, and Elvis Presley.

On a Texas music tour, Lewis and his band had been booked at several night clubs in the Dallas area. While in the Dallas area, his personal bodyguard was charged with murder after shooting a man who was having an affair with his wife. Seeking legal assistance for the bodyguard, Lewis was referred to our law firm by our good friend W. O. Bankston, who had earlier referred Clyde Barrow's sister to our office. The killing happened after the bodyguard learning of his wife's infidelity. He had summoned the "former" friend to a remote area west of Dallas to discuss the alleged affair with his wife. When the man arrived, the bodyguard shot the boyfriend, killing him instantly as he stepped out of his car. The Dallas District Attorney filed capital murder charges, seeking the death penalty. Lewis hired our law firm to defend his bodyguard. Although the jury did return a guilty of murder verdict, we managed to avoid the death penalty when the jury sentenced the bodyguard to a modest term in prison. Lewis invited us to be his guests at each of his concerts while he was in the Dallas area.

The law firm partners also ventured into the night club scene, when the largest dance hall in the Dallas area, "The Plantation Club", became available for lease. It boasted the largest dance floor in Texas at the time – 5000 square feet of hardwood floor located right in the middle of the club. The Plantation Club was located on the south side of the main downtown business district only a few blocks from our office. During our short career as "night club entrepreneurs", we booked several local and regional country bands. The most famous celebrity was Mel Tillis, a nationally known Nashville recording artist who wrote and recorded many top country hit songs during his long career. He was famous for "studdering" when he spoke. Yet when he would begin to sing, the studder disappeared. After a short time, the excitement of hosting celebrity entertainment and staying up late at night got old. Plus, dealing with drunks and breaking up fights didn't go well with the practice of law. So, in the best interest of our health, and marriages, we the club closed after a year.

11

CHAPTER

Dallas, Texas in My Rear-view Mirror

After the Binion case things returned to normal, if that is possible in a law practice. By now, the partners were moving in different directions with our individual practices and personal lives. Without going into details, some marriages and family lives were suffering due in part to the unconventional hours we maintained. The law office was started as a partnership; however, it was never a true partnership. We shared office space and the mutual overhead. Each member maintained his own clients and bank accounts. We would occasionally "co-counsel" on a case, but eventually we closed the office and moved in different directions. Being recently divorced, I was ready for new faces and new places - "Changes in Latitudes, Changes in Attitudes", as the Jimmy Buffett songs goes. I put Dallas in my rear-view mirror, and moved to Fort Lauderdale, Florida. There, I purchased a 42' sailboat which had been built in Norway and sailed to Florida. Appropriately named, "Viking", the owners had explored the west coast of Europe for two years before crossing the Atlantic to America, like Christopher Columbus had done 475 years earlier.

I re-named the boat "Cap'n Sir" and sailed it to the Bahamas Islands and around the Florida east coast. Sitting in the "Red Lion Tavern" in Bimini one evening, I became engaged in a conversation with another tourist named Gene Whatley. I mentioned that I was planning to sail to the Caribbean and needed some additional supplies. Whatley just happened to own a marine store in Cape Coral on the west coast of Florida and offered the supplies at his cost. After returning to Ft. Lauderdale, I contacted Whatley, and he came to Ft. Lauderdale with a friend to help us take "Cap'n Sir" around to the Florida west coast. Our route took us down Florida's east coast, through the Seven Mile Bridge in the middle Florida Keys, then up the west coast to Cape Coral, on the eastern edge of Gulf of Mexico. Gene and Art were driven to Ft. Lauderdale by Gene's older brother, "T-Bone" Whatley, and his lady friend, Maggie.

A few years later, on a sailing trip through the Bahamas, enroute to the Panama Canal, Maggie died after consuming the ship's stove fuel during an alcohol withdrawal seizure. T-Bone had no liquor on the boat, hoping Maggie would "dry out" during the trip. Upon discovering Maggie dead in her bunk, he had no choice but to return to Nassau and report the death to the Bahamian authorities. T-Bone was detained until his brother Gene arrived from Florida, and shortly thereafter the matter was cleared up with the death being ruled "accidental". The Whatleys returned to Cape Coral with Maggie's body, and after the funeral, T-Bone once again set off for the Panama Canal, with Maggie's ashes on board the boat, with nothing but a sextant and the sun and stars for guidance. Unfortunately, as he was nearing the coast of South America, he ran into an extended period of overcast skies, preventing him from taking sun sights. Combined with some strong currents, the boat drifted off course and onto an uncharted reef near the San Blas Islands, just short of the Panama Canal. After several unsuccessful attempts to free himself from the reef, the boat began to break apart from the constant pounding. Reluctantly, he had no choice but to abandon the boat, taking the belongings he could with him and made for a nearby island two miles away. Before leaving the sinking boat, T-Bone poured Maggie's ashes into the ocean and said, "Well, Maggie, I guess this is as far as you go."

This was in the middle of December. Upon reaching the nearby island, T-Bone was greeted by a small tribe of Kuna Indians, native inhabitants on the island. He later learned they were active cannibals, except during a religious holiday when their activities involved celebrating day and night, drinking an alcoholic concoction made from a local guava plant. T-Bone was in luck. At this time of year, they were celebrating Christmas. During the festivities the tribe would drink the "home-brew" until they passed out. When a member would become unconscious, the other members would hoist him up by his feet in a tree until he woke up. They would lower him down and resume the celebration until another member passed out, whereupon the process would repeat itself. Using sign language, T-Bone managed to communicate with the tribal chief whereupon they agreed to take him to a neighboring village to arrange transportation to Panama. Once in Panama, he sent a Western Union message to brother Gene for airfare back to Florida. Immediately upon returning to Cape Coral, T-Bone started construction of a new boat for another attempt to sail to the Canal. Working day and night, thirteen months later T-Bone completed "Sunshine", a 32-foot gaff-rigged sloop built with multiple layers of thick fiberglass. "Sunshine" proved to be capable of the journey. T-Bone and "Sunshine" were now ready for return to the Panama Canal. The Whatleys and I became best friends, enjoying ham radio & sailing for the next 45 years.

After several years and many sailing trips to the Bahamas and the Turks & Caicos Islands, T-Bone finally realized his long-distance sailing days were over, and gave Sunshine to his son-in-law, who had become an avid sailor. A few years later, T-Bone called and said he was planning to build a small bay boat. He asked me if I had any good ideas for a name. I suggested "Sunset", since this would likely be his last boat. Indignant at my comment, he quickly replied, "Why would you think this is my last boat? I'm only

89!" And as always, T-Bone proved to be fit for the task. He built a shallow water bay boat powered by a small electric motor and solar panels. Appropriately, the boat was named "Sunbeam".

Although he was almost totally deaf from a German mortar while serving in WWII, T bone and I kept in touch via amateur radio. Even though he could not hear voices very well, he could hear the high-pitched tones of the Morse Code on the radio. We maintained a radio schedule every Sunday for the next 30 years. On his 90th birthday, I surprised him by walking in with my video camera filming the celebration, as he was relating one of his wild adventures to birthday guests. During the party I took his picture as he climbed his 35 ft radio tower, carrying a large American flag and wearing his WWII Army jacket and boots, with an M-16 carbine slung over his shoulder. Thomas Jefferson "T-Bone" Whatley passed away at the age of 94, having seen more adventures than any person I have ever known.

After spending a couple of years in Cape Coral, I was ready to move on. I returned to Florida's east coast crossing from Fort Myers to Port St. Lucie, then taking the Intercoastal Waterway south to Ft. Lauderdale. Upon reaching Ft. Lauderdale, I had completed a complete circumnavigation of South Florida. However, by now we were ready to move off the boat, so I purchased a small condo with a boat dock and lived there for the next year. Due to the constant maintenance of a wooden boat, I decided to sell "Cap'n Sir", and listed it with a yacht broker in Ft. Lauderdale, and moved back to Texas. A few months later the broker informed me that the "Viking" had been purchased by a friend of Jimmy Buffett. He planned to sail "Cap'n Sir" around the globe, although I never learned if he completed the trip.

12

Return To Texas

Not being sure what I really wanted to do, or where to do it, I returned to Carrollton and reunited with friends. I did some part-time legal work for a friend in his law office. While there, I met two of his "clients". Joe and Jerry, two very personable characters who could charm the horns off a Billy goat. Both had spent time in local jails for various con schemes and hustles. For some reason my friend and his family took a liking to these two characters, and frequently included them in our social activities. To their credit, they never took advantage of our friendship and hospitality.

I had come up with the idea I thought had merit. I started a company manufacturing a portable home bathtub jacuzzi. I had gotten the idea from having sold and serviced vacuum cleaners for short time. The basic component of the jacuzzi was the same pump used in home vacuum cleaners. The output side of the vacuum pump was attached to a soft flexible plastic hose that had multiple small holes and laid on the floor of the bathtub. In order to keep the tube submerged, the tube was filled with small steel ball bearings. The vacuum pump was housed in an attractive brightly painted box and sat outside the tub on the bathroom floor. Being portable, it could be moved from bathroom to bathroom, or even home to home. I named the company "Healthways Hydro Systems". A pretty fancy name for a simple vacuum cleaner motor hooked to a hose. After about a year after the first production, I sold the business to a company in South Carolina. And again, I thought it was time to move on.

Another friend in Carrollton worked for a large insurance company and had become acquainted with a real estate developer from Houston who had relocated to Brownsville, Texas. He had resurrected an old country club and golf course in Brownsville called Valley International Country Club, or "V.I.C.C.", for short. He was now developing a new golf course and country club just north of Brownsville. It was situated on a small ranch covered mostly in grapefruit orchards. The former owner's house was an old colonial mansion previously owned by the widow of silent western movie star, Tom Mix. The new country club would have homes and condos woven in and around a 36-hole golf course. He named it "Rancho Viejo", Spanish for "old ranch".

On a business trip to Brownsville, my friend had an occasion to meet with Rancho Viejo's developer. During a casual conversation, he mentioned that he needed to hire a lawyer to work "in house" for the Rancho Viejo project. My name was mentioned, and the developer asked my friend to have me call him. Upon returning to Dallas, he told me about his conversation with the developer and the possible job opportunity. I called the developer, and he invited me to come to Brownsville to discuss the job. It seemed like a great opportunity for a new adventure. Upon my return to Dallas, we packed our things and moved to Rancho Viejo where we rented a 3-bedroom house on the golf course.

13

"Laid-Back" Rio Grande Valley

The operation of Rancho Viejo consisted of mainly three divisions – the golf course and clubhouse operation, a real estate sales operation, and a construction company. The main idea was to keep the floor plans the same, thereby minimizing the labor and material costs. The homes would be marketed primarily to the wealthy Mexican business community in Matamoros and Monterrey as a second vacation home. Since I was conversant in Spanish, and played golf, I was put with the sales team focusing on the Mexican market. We would invite prospective buyers to visit Rancho Viejo, show them around the property and play a few rounds of golf. Once they arrived, we set them up in a residence and begin entertaining them with golf, lunch, evening cocktails and dinner. During this time, I was playing golf with a prospective home buyer almost daily. Since I was also a pilot, I frequently went along on the sales trips to Monterrey, Mexico and other cities.

Several times a year we would have celebrity guests visit Rancho Viejo. Comedian Phil Harris, singer and professional golfer, Don Cherry and major league baseball star Mickey Mantle were a few of the regulars that would come to Rancho Viejo to perform and enjoy a few days of golf. Since I had played numerous rounds of golf and knew the course well, I was chosen to be their guide and caddie while they were at the club. One memorable highlight occurred during a round when I was assigned to caddie for Mantle. The group included Harris, and a friend of Mantle's. "The Mick" was having a bad round. He could hit a baseball out of the park with regularity, but his golf swing wasn't quite as effective as with a baseball bat. He sprayed the course all morning with golf balls, most of which we never found being lost in a lake, or the orchards. More than once after hitting an errant shot he would "slam" the club into the ground, breaking or severely bending the shaft, rendering the club useless. He was now down to only one long club – a 4 wood. As we approached a particular hole, Mantle, now using the 4 wood as his driver, hit his first tee shot off to the right, out of bounds in tall grass. Teeing up another ball, he proceeded to line drive it deep into the trees on the left. With his frustration at the breaking point, he raised the wood and was about to slam it into the ground, as he had done with the others earlier. At that moment Harris, ever the comedian, cautioned - "Mick, Stop! Hold It! That's your last wood!" ... Everyone but Mantle doubled over laughing.

After several months, the Mexican sales "boom" ended. Bass has become over-extended with his lenders, due to over-spending on ideas that looked good on paper, but never paid off. He was in a vicious circle borrowing money to pay off older loans. As a college finance professor told us in class - "You can't borrow yourself out of debt". I could see the handwriting on the wall. It was time to find a better way to put bread on the table. My first thought was to open a private law office in Brownsville. But since I was not well-known outside Rancho Viejo, I chose my other profession – flying. I was a commercial licensed pilot with multi-engine and instrument ratings. I was qualified to fly for the airlines, but none were hiring at this time, especially in South Texas. So, with the assistance of a friendly local banker, I bought a used Cessna 210, one of the faster single engine airplanes with seating for six people, including the pilot. I arranged to hanger the plane at Southmost Aviation, a local airplane repair facility at the south end of the Brownsville International Airport. The owner and I became friends, and he would hire me to pick up and deliver the various planes he had serviced for his customers. One of his customers was "Mayan Airways", a local charter airline located in Belize, the small country on the western Caribbean coast bordered by Guatemala. Southmost had had been hired by the airline to repaint their fleet of Cessna single engine planes. Although a pilot himself, the shop owner had recently had some health problems and was not legal to fly at this time. So, I was hired to pick up the planes in Belize and fly them back to Brownsville for the service, and then return them to Belize when the work had been completed. The route from Brownsville to Belize went down the west coast of Mexico to Vera Cruz, and across the Bay of Campeche, a 200 mile stretch of open ocean, then further south to the Yucatan Peninsula to Belize City. The trip took two days, with an overnight stop at Vera Cruz.

For the past century, Great Britain and Guatemala had been fighting over who rightfully owned Belize. On one of my trips, I unknowingly arrived during the middle of a minor skirmish between the Guatemalan and British armies, and the British forces had recently secured control of the Belize airport. On one trip after landing, the control tower instructed me to taxi to a restricted parking area and was immediately approached by a British special forces officer who advised me of the situation. After explaining my purpose for landing in Belize, I was advised that my plane would be under military guard, until I was ready to depart with the Mayan Airways plane. After repeating this routine a few times, the British officer and I became acquainted. We would sit in the airport cafe, enjoying a cup of coffee and discuss how the "war" was progressing. After a few weeks, Southmost finished repainting the last Mayan plane, and my flying life returned to normal ... for a short period of time.

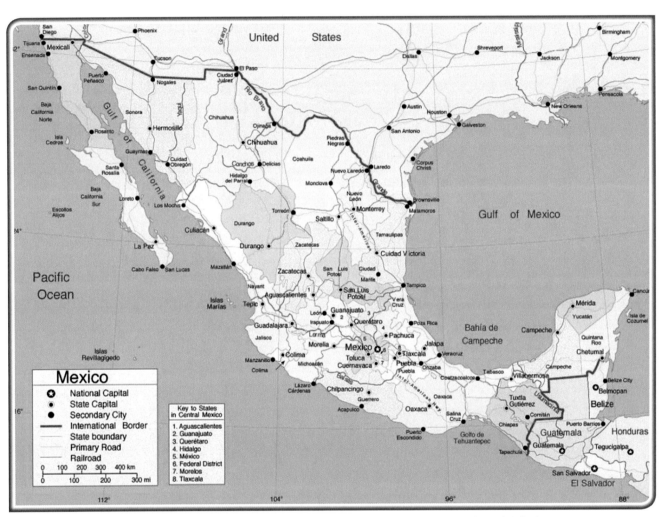

(*Mexico's east coast. Bahia de Campeche, Yucatan Peninsula, Guatemala and Belize*)

14

Here We Are in The Tijuana Jail (Kingston Trio, 1958)

During my days at Rancho Viejo, I had become friends with a Mexican businessman, Ricardo Duran, who lived in Brownsville, but his office was in Matamoros, Mexico, across the International Bridge at Brownsville. He was an "Agente de Aduanas Commercial", a commercial customs agent, and prepared the paperwork and arranged for the crossing of commercial trucks between Mexico and Texas at the International Bridge at Brownsville. His clients were Mexican businessmen scattered throughout Mexico. Ricardo and I soon became good friends and would often spend our afternoons after work at a local bar in Matamoros, the "Agua Viva", socializing with his friends. Although some spoke English, Spanish was the preferred language. I was usually the only "gringo" but could carry on a decent conversation in Spanish. Ricardo was always a jokester, and he would wager for a round of drinks with his friends on my ability to read the Spanish newspaper. These were fun times, and it soon became a daily ritual for Ricardo and me, along with friends, to meet after work at the Agua Viva for refreshments and lively conversation. It wasn't long before I was flying Ricardo around northern Mexico on business trips to solicit his customs brokerage contracts. One such trip stands out above the rest.

A very prominent Mexican businessman from Monterrey contacted Duran, asking if he knew anyone with an airplane available for private charter. His son had been on South Padre Island for the past week, celebrating "Semana Santa", the Mexican holy week during Easter, and it was time for him to return home to resume school. Duran gave me the businessman's number and I contacted the father and was hired to transport his son, and the father's personal pilot from Brownsville to Monterrey. The father had a small, single engine airplane; however, his pilot was not qualified for flying in bad weather. He had no instrument flying experience, and the weather forecast between Brownsville and Monterrey warned of the possibility of heavy thunderstorms. He would leave the plane in Brownsville and pick it up later. Brownsville to Monterrey is about 170 air miles ... about an hour flight in my plane.

Upon arriving at Southmost Aviation, I noticed a small stack of boxes in the hangar next to my plane. Two young men were standing by the boxes. One introduced himself as the Mexican businessman's son, and the other young man was his father's personal pilot. These were my passengers for the trip to Monterrey. I checked the weather, and it would be "marginal", but I felt like we could make the trip without a problem. The plane was fueled, and ready to depart. When I asked the son what was in the boxes, he replied, "Stereos. One for me and one for my sister." I told him that we would have to stop at the Matamoros airport to clear customs. Something I would not have done had it not been for the "extra freight". This later proved to be a mistake. Looking back, I should have taken my chances at the Monterrey airport. Had there had been a problem, I'm certain the father would have been able to take care of it. But I decided to follow the rules, and we hopped over the Rio Grande River from Brownsville to the Matamoros airport. After landing, I taxied to the public parking area where we were greeted by a customs official. Speaking in Spanish, I informed him that we were on our way to Matamoros. He inquired what was in the boxes, and I told them it was stereo equipment belonging to my passenger, and that I was flying him to Monterrey after his spring break vacation on South Padre Island. The agent asked me to wait in the coffee shop and he would return shortly. He and the son went to another area, leaving me and the pilot in the cafe. After a few minutes, the agent returned with another agent and informed me that we had to go with them. When I asked if there was a problem, without responding, they escorted me to a car, and never explained where we were going. They drove about 15 miles to the Mexican Customs office in Matamoros, where we were escorted to a small room, with no chairs. A middle age American woman was standing in the room. She told us that she had been arrested because they found some baby products in the trunk of her car. She told us this wasn't her first arrest, and that they would routinely take the contraband, and release her back at the border. She said the Customs officials would let her call brother in San Antonio to wire money for her fine and offered to have him call my wife and advise her of my detention. Taking her up on the offer, I gave her my wife's name and our phone number in Brownsville. I asked her to tell her brother to have my wife call Ricardo Duran in Brownsville, and advise him of my situation, knowing he would contact the father to get me released. I later learned that the woman's brother did in fact called my wife and told her that he had just received a call from his sister, and that she and I were in custody together at the Mexican Customs facility. I thought, "Now how will I explain this to my wife!"

After what seemed like an eternity, they escorted the son and pilot out and I never saw them again. After more waiting, I was finally escorted out of the room down a hallway to another office. As we approached, I noticed the door was closed and the agent escorting me pointed and instructed me to go inside. By this time, I knew something was seriously wrong. I was hesitant to open the door, not knowing what was on the other side. But the agent kept pointing to the door, and insisting I open it. Turning the knob, I slowly opened the door. Immediately, several flashes went off, momentarily blinding me. It was reporters from the local Matamoros newspaper, "El Mundo". The following day my picture was on the front page, with a startled expression on my face, as if I had just seen a ghost. Beside me in the picture were the stereo cartons. The newspaper headline read – *"Contrabandista Americano detenido con 3 mil pesos de electronicos."* Translated in English – *"American smuggler detained with 3 million pesos in contraband electronics."* I was then escorted to another room where the "Comandante", or chief of customs was seated. "Captain Marroquin" was dressed in a neatly pressed uniform, covered with an assortment of medals and badges indicating his rank and importance. He asked me where I was going with the electronics. I explained they belonged to the young man they had detained with me at the airport, and that I was simply flying him and the other pilot to Monterrey for his father because he didn't think his pilot was qualified to fly in bad weather. After a short exchange, Marroquin accused me of smuggling electronics into the country. However, I would be released if I agreed to sign over the title to my plane and leave it with him. When I refused, he returned me to the holding room. Later I was transported to the larger prison and placed in the general population with an assortment of criminals. I noticed one particular mean-looking Mexican eyeing my Rolex watch, and demanded I give it to him. He told me if I didn't hand it over, I would have to clean the bathroom. It was not a nice place. Another American prisoner approached me and introduced himself. He told me the tough guy was considered the *"capo"*, or "chief", and the guards allowed him to run the cell block. He had been convicted of murder and was serving a lengthy term in prison. His nickname was "Matillo", Spanish for "hammer", the weapon he had used to kill his victim. The Rolex was given to me by my father when I graduated from law school, and I wasn't about to part with it. I decided to stand my ground with Matillo. As it turned out he was more "bluster" than "brawn". I told him he would have to take it from me, but it would be after the fight. Fortunately, he backed off.

I spent the next three days in this cell block. My wife was able to contact Ricardo, as he showed up on the second day and told me that he had contacted the father, and they were working on my release. The father was a prominent Mexican businessman and owned most of the railroad box cars in Mexico, and a personal friend of the Mexican President, Jose Lopez Portillo advised his Attorney General to contact the deputy Attorney General in Matamoros with instructions to release me and my plane as quickly as possible. *"As quickly as possible"* in Mexico was 7 more days. However, while waiting for my release I was moved from the prison to more civilized quarters at the Ritz Hotel in downtown Matamoros. Although still technically under arrest, I was allowed to go out to eat, shop, or just walk around, but I was always escorted by two plainclothes Mexican guards. They even allowed me to cross the bridge and spend the night at home in Rancho Viejo, as long as I returned the next morning for "bed check". They surely knew I would return to pick up my plane, once it was officially released. And they were absolutely correct in that assumption. Over the next week, the guards and I became friendly, and even went to a movie together one afternoon.

It was Sunday, June 15, 1975. Father's Day. My wife came over and we dined at the Drive Inn, a very popular restaurant in Matamoros, reminiscent of Rick's Cafe in the famous Humphrey Bogart movie "Casablanca". Shortly thereafter, I was transported to the Federal Prosecutor's office. He presented me with some documents, all in Spanish, and asked me to sign them. He said it was the official release for me and my plane. Not trusting my understanding of Spanish legalese, I requested that my agent friend, Duran, be called to translate the document. After carefully reading the document, he said it was an official release for me and my plane. After signing the papers, the Mexican Federal Attorney asked if I knew how to fly a Cessna 310, a twin engine, eight passenger plane. I replied that I had flown them several times. He had recently confiscated one from a drug dealer and needed a pilot and offered me a job as his personal pilot. My friend and I just looked at each other, dumbfounded. There, in a few short minutes, I had gone from being a prisoner of the Mexican government, to the chief prosecutor's personal pilot! Only in Mexico! I politely thanked him for the offer, but respectfully declined, telling him I was reminded of the mouse who had been caught in the trap. I didn't want any more cheese. I just wanted out! We thanked him for his courtesies, and headed for the airport, and my plane. Anxious to get back across the Rio Grande to Texas. However, this was not the end of my Mexico flying. I continued flying around the country regularly. I had mortgage payments to make, and Texas charters were not as lucrative as in Mexico. A few years later, after the Customs incident, I learned that Captain Marroquin had been arrested and imprisoned for smuggling. He was ultimately murdered by some of the very prisoners he had put there. An appropriate ending for his kind.

A few days after my release, my friend contacted me and said he had someone he wanted me to meet. I was introduced to a short, stocky Mexican gentleman who was the commanding officer of the "Mexican Federales", the federal police force for the entire State of Tamaulipas, the largest state in Mexico stretching from Matamoros west to Nuevo Laredo, and south to Tampico. He needed a private plane to transport supplies and equipment to Ciudad Victoria in the southern part of the state. His police force was conducting surveillance of an illegal trucking operation suspected of transporting merchandise (not drugs) from the area to Matamoros and crossing it into the U.S. border in Brownsville. He had a list of supplies that his team needed. Ricardo was going to purchase them in Brownsville, and then we would fly them to Ciudad Victoria. Another opportunity for me to work for the Mexican government! The list consisted of cartons of flashlight batteries, hand tools, believe it or not, cases of ammunition. The back seats of my plane had to be removed in order to make room for the freight.

With Duran in the co-pilot seat, we took off for Ciudad Victoria, about an hour and half flight. I had been instructed not clear Customs in Matamoros, nor upon my arrival in Ciudad Victoria. This was an "off the record" mission. My flight in and out of the country had already been approved. Upon landing at the Ciudad Victoria airport, we were met by the Chief Federale officer and a small group of uniformed Mexican soldiers. They instructed me to park the plane in a particular location and proceeded to unload the cartons of supplies into a military vehicle and placing a guard by the plane. We were then escorted to a waiting car, and driven to a local hotel in town, where we were treated to a nice lunch. I later learned that the operation was successful, and they arrested the traffickers. The next day, Duran and I flew back to Brownsville.

My charter service was picking up, but I learned that some people weren't exactly comfortable in a single engine aircraft, especially when the weather is marginal. I decided to look for a twin-engine aircraft and located one in Houston – an Aero Commander 500B, a rugged aircraft that carried 6 passengers with a large baggage compartment. It wasn't as fast as the Cessna 210, but it was much roomier, and more stable in rough weather. The owner was a successful business owner in Houston moving to a larger plane. His personal banker agreed to finance the plane. I returned to Brownsville with the new plane and resumed my charter service. I made several trips around northern Mexico in the next few months. However, the charter business was still not producing enough money to cover my flying expenses. When a friend in Dallas called offering me a job flying for his new company in the Fort Worth suburb of Arlington, we decided it was time to move back to our old hometown. We settled in the Dallas suburb of Farmers Branch, not far from my original hometown of Carrollton. I had made another complete circle in my residence locations. The years spent at Ranch Viejo, and Brownsville were memorable and full of adventure for sure. I met a lot of interesting people and developed a fondness for South Texas, and as the reader will later learn, they were a major factor in my return years later.

15

Meanwhile ... Back at the Ranch

My friend in Dallas had started the new company about the time we decided to take the job at Rancho Viejo. He had previously retired from Radio Shack, the national consumer electronics company as the national marketing manager, personally involved in establishing the Radio Shack franchises throughout the United States. He was a visionary and foresaw the Citizens Band - "CB"- radio boom coming. He started a manufacturing and marketing company building CB antennas and accessories. "Breaker Corporation", the company name, was a reference to the well-known trucker expression, "Breaker, Breaker 19", which was the customary call for CB radio operators wishing to chat with others, especially over-the-road truck drivers. I wore three hats with Breaker Corporation. My primary job was as company pilot, flying the owner and other company personnel around the country. I was also the "in-house attorney". But the company decided to expand from the CB antenna market into amateur radio, so I was naturally included in the discussion about the design and features of the new radio. The director of our marketing at Breaker had met and became friends with William Halligan, the founder of Hallicrafters Radio, who, along with Art Collins of Collins Radio, were legends in the amateur and military communications field. Bill Halligan was retired and living in Florida, after selling his company to Northrup Corporation. At this time Northrup was selling instrument landing systems and commercial flight avionics to the U. S. military and wasn't using the Hallicrafters name. They readily agreed to sell the Hallicrafters company and name to Breaker Corporation. I might note here that one of my first radios as a youngster, when I first became interested in amateur radio, was a Hallicrafters shortwave receiver. Now I was about to meet Mr. Halligan, himself, one of my childhood heroes, and be a part of the resurrection of the legendary Hallicrafters brand. We contacted a Japanese electronics manufacturing company in Tokyo, where two of the marketing department members and I were sent to establish the production of a "Hallicrafters" amateur radio transceiver. Unfortunately, our time in the amateur radio field was short-lived, as the competition with the three established world leaders in shortwave radios - Kenwood, Icom, and Yaesu - was too much for a small regional company like Breaker Corporation to compete with, and the production of the Hallicrafters radios ended after a couple of years. However, I was fortunate to have met, played golf, and become personal friends with one of my childhood heroes – William "Mister Bill" Halligan. We continued to keep in touch via amateur radio after he returned to Florida, until his passing years later.

(William Halligan and author in front of Breaker Corporation offices, circa 1975)

(Hallicrafters shortwave receiver)

After the production of Hallicrafters ended, I spent most of my time flying the company owner and friends, and Breaker customers to Mustang Island, near Corpus Christi, where he owned a vacation home, and docked his 42' offshore fishing boat. The boat's name was "Breaker", as one might guess. We also took a couple of trips to Cozumel, Mexico looking for a dock space for "Breaker" during the marlin fishing season. This never panned out as most of the dockage was either reserved or unsatisfactory for the boat. On one exploratory trip, as I was approaching Cozumel, I radioed the airport authorities that control landing at Isla Mujeres, a small town on the mainland, across the bay from Cozumel. I advised them that I was inbound, and requested permission to land, but that I couldn't locate the runway. The reply was that there was no airport, per se, but that I could land on the main street in town, and they asked how much runway I needed. I was advised they would place two police cars on each end to block off Main Street for me to land, and then be escorted to a local bank parking lot where I could park my plane. When I was ready to depart, I called the police station and the process was put in place again, I took off literally from downtown Isla Mujeres! What Service! Only in Mexico!

I sold the Aero Commander to Breaker Corporation, and I returned to work at the trucking company. A few years later the CB boom played out, and Breaker Corporation was sold to Motorola Corporation. By this time Hunsaker Trucking had three terminals in Texas, located in Dallas, Houston, and Tyler. The company owned a twin-engine Beechcraft E-18, which was a much larger plane than the Aero Commander with room for 5 passengers, plus the pilot and co-pilot. A total of seven persons. We had a full-time professional captain, and I flew co-pilot. Dad always like the idea of having two engines, and two pilots!

16

Texas Politics

Dad was always involved with supporting his favorite political candidates, and he became personal friends with most of them. He would offer the use of the company plane for their campaign travels around the state. I always went along as co-pilot, and a representative of the company. Some of the notable people we flew were Texas Lt. Governor Ben Barnes, University of Texas head football coach, Darrell Royal, and Lady Bird Johnson's personal secretary, Liz Carpenter. On one particular flight from San Angelo, Texas back to Austin, where we flew Ms. Carpenter to attend a special awards ceremony naming her "Person of the Year" by the Texas Chamber of Commerce, we lost partial power in one of the engines. The pilot and I were worried that if the passengers became aware of the situation they might panic, so I went to check on Ms. Carpenter and her associate. I asked Ms. Carpenter if they would care for a beverage or a snack. Meanwhile, the captain continued to nurse the bad engine, and we eventually landed safely at the Austin Municipal Airport. Neither Ms. Carpenter, nor her companion, never realized we had flown most of the return trip on one engine.

In addition to Governor Preston Smith, and Lt. Governor Ben Barnes, another Texas politico figure we flew was Speaker of the Texas House, Gus Mutscher. Smith, Barnes and Mutscher were the State's three highest elected officials from 1969 to 1973. Mutscher and Barnes were ultimately forced to leave office because they had been involved in the infamous Sharpstown Bank Scandal. The scandal revolved around Houston banker and insurance company manager Frank Sharp and his companies, the Sharpstown State Bank and the National Bankers Life Insurance Corporation. Sharp granted loans from his bank to state officials who would, in turn, purchase stock in National Bankers Life, to be resold later at a huge profit, after Sharp artificially inflated the company's value. One of the victims of the scandal, Strake Jesuit College Preparatory, lost $6,000,000 and a portion of the school's land following the advice of Sharp. Using the stock as encouragement, Sharp pushed for legislation that would benefit

National Bankers Life, increasing the value of the company to its investors—the very people who would push the legislation through. The scheme succeeded in generating profits for the investors on the order of a quarter of a million dollars, but the U.S. Securities and Exchange Commission stepped in early in 1971, filing criminal and civil charges against former state attorney general Waggoner Carr, former state insurance commissioner John Osorio, Frank Sharp, and a number of others.

By the middle of 1971, anyone in the state government who might have been connected to Sharp was heavily pressured politically. Allegations of bribery to push favorable bills through the legislature spread to House Speaker Gus Mutscher, Lieutenant Governor Ben Barnes, and even Governor Preston Smith. Osorio was convicted of embezzling $641,000 from an insurance company's pension fund. A court had decided that he had wrongly used money lent by Dallas Bank and Trust Co. to the National Bankers Life Employees Pension Fund to buy stock in National Bankers Life Insurance Co. of Dallas. Osorio was sentenced to three years but served only 14 months. House Speaker Gus Mutscher also was indicted. He resigned in 1972 after being convicted but was able to avoid serving any prison time. Texas Attorney General Waggoner Carr also was charged in the scandal. Gov. Preston Smith avoided conviction, but was labeled an UN-indicted co-conspirator, and rising political star Ben Barnes, who was elected Texas lieutenant governor at the age of 30, was drawn in by unproven allegations, which proved to be enough to make his gubernatorial dreams falter. Years later, Osorio hit the jackpot. Choosing the numbers 1, 16, 36, 43, 44 and 52 in the state lottery in 2000, Osorio and his then-girlfriend, later-wife took home $21 million after taxes. Years later, Dad's friend, W. O. Bankston, who had referred Clyde Barrow's sister to my law office, referred John Osorio to me for representation on an unrelated charge.

Ben Barnes
State Speaker of the House 1965-1969
Lieutenant Governor 1969-1973

17

Rubbing Elbows with Miss America

The 1969 Texas vs. Arkansas football game, sometimes referred to as the "Game of the Century", was played on December 6 in which No. 1 Texas visited No. 2 Arkansas at Razorback Stadium in Fayetteville, Arkansas. The Longhorns came back from a 14–0 deficit after three quarters to win 15–14. President Richard Nixon attended the game and established it as a national championship game by announcing he would award the winning team a presidential plaque declaring them ***"The number-one college football team in college football's one-hundredth year."*** With a Nielsen rating of 52.1 (a 74% share), this was, and remains as of 2023, the highest TV rating in American football history, college or professional. And I was there.

We flew Gus Mutscher and his wife Donna Axum to the Arkansas/Texas football game in the Hunsaker company plane, and I was invited to go to the game as their guests. Donna Axum had been a celebrity at the University of Arkansas in 1964 when she won the Miss Arkansas pageant – then a month later was crowned Miss America, the first Arkansan to win the title. She was, of course, an ardent Razorback fan, and Mutscher, being from Texas, rooted for the Longhorns. We had seats on the 50-yard line, about 15 rows up, as I recall. Mutscher was seated on one side of me, and "Miss America" on the other. To this day, I still remember cheering for each team when one would score or make a big play! I was rubbing elbows with "Miss America", and one of the most powerful elected officials in Texas. A very memorable event in my life. The prior conviction for his involvement in the Sharpstown Bank scandal had been reversed, restoring his right to hold public office. He was elected County Judge of Washington

County where the county seat was in his hometown of Brenham. Several years later, I happened to be in Brenham, and walked into a restaurant. At a small table across from me sat Mutscher. I walked over and asked, "Mr. Mutscher, you may not remember me. I'm Brian Hunsaker." He immediately stood up, shook my hand and said, "My Lord. Of course I do. You flew me and Donna to the Arkansas/Texas national championship game." Gus Mutscher died on February 26, 2023, at the age of 90 in Brenham, Texas. Donna Axum died on November 4, 2018, at age 76 in Fort Worth, Texas, from complications of <u>Parkinson's disease.</u>

Donna Axum

Gus Mustcher

18

The Turks & Caicos Islands

By 1978 I had become bored with Dallas again. I needed another adventure. The sailing bug was still biting. But this time I intended to sail the entire eastern Caribbean from Florida to Trinidad. My plan was to travel the islands for 3 months, then leave the boat in a secure harbor, and return home for 6 months. Then repeat the process until I reached the north coast of South America. After that, I wasn't sure. Most likely, I would sell the boat, and return home, having completed my dream voyage. It took a while to convince my father for a "leave of absence" from the company, but he eventually gave in, probably thinking he had no choice, knowing me and my determination to do something when I set my mind to it. With my wife, son Kerry, and a stepdaughter, we drove to Tampa, Florida, where I had located the perfect boat for the voyage. It was a 42' fiberglass ketch with a small inboard engine, made by Gulfstar Yachts, a relatively new boat manufacturer. I named the boat "Honeysuckle", which was suggested by the wife of my Dallas friend who had introduced me to the Rancho Viejo developer years before. It was a nickname she had given me years earlier.

My plan was to sail down the west coast of Florida from Tampa to Cape Coral, reuniting with my old boating pals, Gene and T-Bone Whatley, while I provisioned the boat for the extended voyage south. Cape Coral has always been one of my favorite places, especially for boating. Gene Whatley still owned his marine store, and every day was filled with socializing with friends, and boating activities. Leaving there was difficult. But if I was to make any progress south to the Caribbean in the next 3 months, I had to move on. So, after a few weeks getting the boat ready, and fun with our Cape Coral friends, we headed south for Marathon in the Florida Keys – our planned "jump off" spot for the trip across the gulf stream to the Bahamas. Our first port of call was Bimini, where had originally met Gene Whatley on our first voyage to the Bahamas in "Cap'n Sir" several yeas earlier. Bimini is the closest Bahama Island from Florida and was the popular hangout of Ernest Hemingway when he was on the hunt for the elusive blue marlin. After a few days in Bimini, we headed southeast to the capital city of Nassau, then down the Exumas chain of islands south to Georgetown, one of the largest settlements in the Exumas, and a good place to rest and replenish our supplies, before making the open passage to Crooked and Acklins, remote islands at the southeastern edge of the Bahamas, where food, fuel and supplies were scarce. Next stop was Mayaguana, the farthermost eastern Bahamian island. From here the next closest harbor was West Caicos, in the British-owned protectorate of the Turks & Caicos Islands.

While we were in Georgetown, I had met a sailor who noticed my radio antenna and ask if I was a ham radio operator. Acknowledging I was, we struck up a nice conversation about ham radio. When he asked where I was headed, I replied, "Puerto Rico, and down the West Indies chain. At this point I wasn't sure which route I would take going south. I only had two choices. Go south toward Great Inagua in the Bahamas, or southeast toward Turks & Caicos. When he suggested the Turks & Caicos route, I was surprised, because everything I had read in the cruising guides about the T & Cs was not good. They had a reputation of being unfriendly to strangers, especially those that arrived by boat, which at this time was the only way to get there, unless you owned your own airplane. He had been there, and assured me the cruising guides were mistaken, and that the Turks & Caicos were perfectly safe. He convinced me it would be the best choice for this leg of my journey. After several days in Georgetown, we set sail for the Turks & Caicos Islands, going east to Crooked and Acklins Islands, and finally Mayaguana – our last anchorage before crossing to the Turks & Caicos at West Caicos, a small island at the western edge of the T & Cs.

It is customary with cruising yachtsmen to travel in company with one or more boats for a number of reasons. Safety being the primary one, especially when you're in a remote area of a foreign country. Our first stop after leaving Nassau was Norman's Cay, a popular anchorage in the northern Exumas chain. There we met two young Canadians, Jamie and Rob, who were on a one-year sabbatical, having sailed their 25 ft. sailboat, "Hobbit", from Windsor, Canada to the Bahamas. We sailed together for the next few weeks, finally parting ways after spending a week together in Cap Haitian, on the north coast of Haiti. Haiti (the country) shares the island of Hispaniola with the Dominican Republic. Haiti occupies approximately one fourth of the western part of the island, and Dominican Republic is on the remaining three-fourths of the island on the east. Cap Haitian, on the north coast of Haiti has an interesting history. In the early 1800s, it had proclaimed its independence from France, and Henri Christophe, who was a leader in the war for Haitian independence (1791-1804) later proclaimed himself President (1807-11), and ultimately self-proclaimed King Henri I (1811-20) of northern Haiti. Christophe was paranoid and had lingering fears that the French would return to reclaim the country and have him exiled. It became such an obsession that he decided to build a giant fort on the top of the highest peak, just outside Cap Haitian. Using slave labor carrying large granite blocks to the top of the mountain, it took 13 years, and the loss of hundreds of Haitian lives to finally complete "The Citadel". Two hundred years later, the cannons, and cannon balls are still sitting in place, ready to defend Cap Haitian from an invasion that never happened. The French never came. The "Hobbits", Rob and Jamie, were continuing on south to the Caribbean. We said our goodbyes and parted company at Cap Haitian. Unfortunately, we were out of time, so we returned to Providenciales and docked "Honeysuckle" at the marina for the next several months and returned home to Dallas.

(The Citadel fortress and cannons near Cap Haitian)

(La Badie, Haiti. S/V "Hobbit", foreground; S/V "Honeysuckle, background)

The friendly sailor in Georgetown had also given me the name of another American who was living on his boat at West Caicos with his wife and a young son. He and his wife had been the sole inhabitants of West Caicos for a couple of years and would be helpful navigating the coral reefs around the Caicos Islands. As luck would have it, they were both ham radio operators. Radio contact was made as I approached the northwestern tip of Providenciales. With his guidance, I was able to stay in deep water, and made it safely to a nice anchorage on the south side of West Caicos. A year later, upon returning to Providenciales and "Honeysuckle", the couple and I were reunited. The "marina project" was still unfinished, and not much had changed since my previous visit. After spending a few days at West Caicos, and given a tour of the island, we needed to re-supply the boat with food, water and fuel, so we moved over to the west end of Providenciales ("Provo", as the natives say), and anchored at Sapodilla

Bay near a white sand beach, and within walking distance of South Dock, a commercial shipping dock. There, I borrowed a car for the short drive to the grocery store.

Providenciales is the western most populated (not counting the one family on West Caicos) in the Turks & Caicos chain, stretching from Grand Turk (the capital) on the east end to West Caicos on the west. "Provo" is shaped much like a banana with the ends at the top. (a real "banana republic") The "downtown", or commercial section, is located approximately in the center of the upturned "banana". At this time there was only a single lane caliche road extending from Northwest Point, at the furthermost northwest end (think left tip of banana) to "Leeward Going Through" on the east end (right tip of banana). "Downtown" is approximately halfway (at bottom of banana). A couple miles from downtown on the north coast is a protected harbor - Seller's Pond, where the Third Turtle Inn and Marina were located. This would be a safe and secure place to leave "Honeysuckle" for a few months. After leaving West Caicos, we took the boat around the north coast of "Provo", and was guided through yet another treacherous reef, and dropped anchor in Sellers Pond. "There I met an "expatriated" American, Doc Withey, and his wife and two sons, who had moved to Providenciales from Michigan a few years earlier. He managed the marina for a group of American investors that had built the "Third Turtle Inn", a small hotel, with a restaurant and bar. He and his sons agreed to take care of "Honeysuckle" while we were in Texas.

19

Back in Texas

Once we returned back home, we settled into our old routines – work, school, and a "normal" lifestyle. It was a big adjustment, after 3 months on a small boat on a big ocean, going from one interesting spot to another. Our two children that had been with us on the boat had been "home-schooling" since we left Texas. And now was probably a good time for them to get back to a more structured schooling and be with other children their age. For the next several months, we settled into a normal routine of work and socializing with the friends we hadn't seen the past 6 months. One such friend, an attorney with whom I had been associated with after my previous law firm dissolved, had also left the law practice and ventured into the night club business. He had bought a very popular club in Dallas called "Whiskey River", named after the song, and formerly owned by the famous country music legend, Willie Nelson. One of the performers at the club was a country songwriter named Alex Harvey. Harvey had become well-known in the music circles having written the hit songs - "Delta Dawn", recorded by Tanya Tucker, and "Reuben James", sung by Kenny Rogers. Harvey attended some of our social gatherings, and at one party I mentioned that I had tried my hand at song writing. Harvey then asked me sing one for him. We went into another room away from the party noise, and with my guitar for accompaniment, I sang a couple of my originals. After I finished the songs, he complimented me, and offered to help get one he particularly liked published and recorded in Nashville. For various reasons, this never materialized, and I lost contact with Harvey after he left the Dallas area and moved back to his original home in Kentucky.

During our time in Dallas, I stayed in regular contact with my friend at West Caicos via ham radio, and he would relay information back and forth between me and Withey concerning my boat. After about 8 months in Dallas, I was ready to go back to Provo, and resume my cruise. However, getting from Dallas back to Provo wasn't as simple as getting from Provo to Dallas. When we left Provo, we were able to hitch a ride with a friend I had met that had a private plane and made regular runs to a small airfield in Lantana, Florida. Scheduling my return on a commercial airline from Dallas to Florida, then getting from either Ft. Lauderdale or West Palm Beach, then over to the small airfield in Lantana at the same time my friend would be there, was going to be a challenge to organize. By this time, Dad had accepted the situation and was willing to help, I'm sure thinking it would be much safer for all if he had a hand in the operation. So, after some discussion, it was decided that the company would buy a small airplane for my trips to the boat, and in between it would be used in Dallas for the frequent business trips to the company office in Tyler, about 120 miles east. The plane we decided on was a 5 place, single engine, Beechcraft Bonanza. It had an airspeed of over 175 mph. I was able to leave Dallas at sunup, and make Provo before dark, with one stop for re-fueling in Florida, weather permitting.

We arrived in the late afternoon at the Provo airstrip, a 2500' stretch of hard-packed caliche which had been bulldozed on a relatively flat stretch of land in the mid-1970s by the original developer, Fritz Ludington, from Florida. Ludington had previously built a small resort in Georgetown called" The Two Turtle Inn". After successfully completing The Two Turtle Inn, he began searching for a suitable location for his next resort. He had spotted Providenciales accidentally while searching the outlying Bahamas islands south of the Exumas. Originally a part of the Bahamas, the Turks & Caicos Islands had chosen to remain a British possession after the Bahamas declared their independence from Great Britain in July 1973. Knowing this, Ludington flew to Grand Turk, the capital and negotiated a deal with the Turks government to begin development of Providenciales. He was given 4000 acres of land on Provo in return for his agreement to develop the island. Ludington sent two of his associates – Bengt Soderqvist and Tommy Coleman. Soderqvist was a licensed surveyor originally from Sweden and worked for Ludington on the Two Turtle Inn development in the Bahamas. Soderqvist was also married to the daughter of a Michigan developer, a major financial backer of Ludington. Tommy Coleman had been associated with Ludington in his early developments in Florida, before going to the Bahamas. Not a professional of any trade, Coleman was a natural born comedian, and entertainer, and could bring laughter instantaneously with his comical witticisms and jokes. He was also an erstwhile singer and guitar player. Years later, after my return to Provo as the manager of the Third Turtle Inn, Tommy and I became close friends. After the guests had finished dinner, Tommy and I would put on an impromptu "Bud Abbott and Lou Costello" comedy routine, with me playing the straight, "Bud Abbott" role, and Tommy, the comedian "Lou Costello". We became affectionately known at the Inn as "Bud and Stud". We had T-shirts printed for the comedy routine. On my shirt it said, "I'm Bud, and He's Stud", with the index finger pointing toward Tommy, who would be standing on my left. Tommy's T-Shirt was just the reverse, saying "I'm Stud, and He's Bud", with his index finger pointing to me on the right. Over the next few years, our comedy routines became quite popular, albeit our "fan club" was limited to the guests staying at the Inn.

Upon returning to Provo, my plan had been to prepare the boat to continue the trip south to the Caribbean. That all changed one evening while I was sitting in the open-air bar of the Third Turtle. It was empty, except for me and the bartender, an immigrant from Haiti, who spoke good English. He was strumming a guitar, and singing to himself, and having trouble with the words and chords of Willie Nelson song. I sat down at the bar and introduced myself, and asked if I could borrow the guitar. I began to play and sing the Willie song Eddie had been fumbling with. Being an open-air bar, and near the restaurant, and cabins, it wasn't long before I had attracted small crowd. They began ordering drinks and singing along. By 9:00 the bar was packed, and I was swamped with requests for numerous songs. Eddie told me he hadn't seen this bar that busy in a long time and asked me to come back the next night. For the next several nights, I was a regular at the bar. Word of the live entertainment, and the increase in bar patrons soon spread around the hotel and marina. Withey had heard about the music and mentioned it to the Third Turtle Inn owner, Richard DuPont. DuPont was an heir of the famous Dupont family from Delaware and had been an original investor with Fritz Ludington when the Third Turtle Inn was first built. Dupont had purchased the Inn from Ludington a few years prior to Ludington's passing. One morning, Withey came to me at the boat, and told me that Dupont wanted to meet me. Apparently, he had gotten word of the increase of business at the bar from Withey. We walked to the tennis courts the next morning, where Dupont was playing tennis with his wife, and I was introduced to Dupont. He shook my hand and thanked me for helping improve the bar attendance. I told him it was as much fun for me as it was for everyone else, and I was happy I could help. He explained that he was not happy with his current manager, a transplanted Dutchman with a brusque personality and unpopular with the guests. After some discussion about his plans for the hotel and bar, Dupont offered me the job as manager of the Third Turtle Inn, and my wife as assistant manager. We would be furnished a residence at the Inn, a small house sitting on a cliff, overlooking the Inn and the marina, plus all living expenses, including meals, and drinks, and a $18,000 a year salary. A very tempting offer, since I had always dreamed of living in the Caribbean and becoming a full-time author. However, I was already making over $50,000 at the trucking company, living in a 4-bedroom home on a country club golf course in Dallas. I had a tough decision to make. I told Dupont I would think about it, and discuss it with my wife, and get back to him in a couple of days. He said he would see me later that evening at the bar. He wanted to hear the music. That one chance meeting with Dupont changed my cruising plans. I was now considering a new adventure. Once back in Dallas I was naturally apprehensive of my imminent meeting with my father to discuss my *"changes in latitude, changes in attitude"* plan. Surprisingly, the meeting went fairly well. No blood was shed. I think knowing that I would be working for a Dupont, Dad was more comfortable about my leaving Dallas and the company. Ultimately, the house was sold, and we packed all the personal items we were taking back to Provo. The rest was either stored, or sold, and we took a commercial flight to Florida, and met Dupont at his stateside office in Florida. We flew back to Providenciales Dupont's personal plane and took over as manager of The Third Turtle Inn and applied for permanent resident status in the Turks & Caicos Islands. The next 5 years would probably be the most exciting and enjoyable in my life up to now.

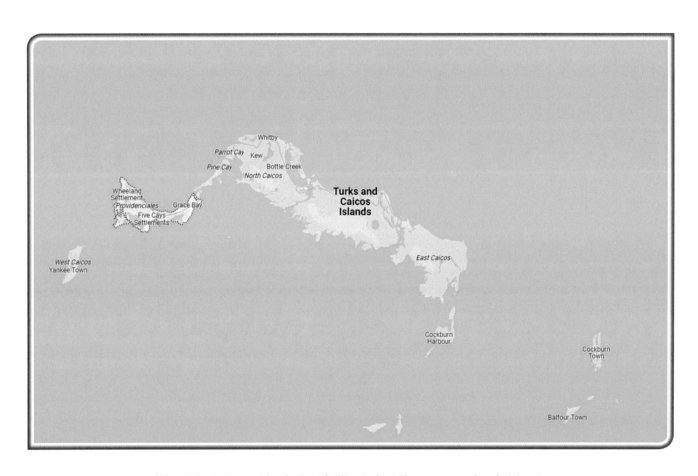

(*The Turks & Caicos Islands, British West Indies. Photo courtesy Google Maps.*)

20

"Permanent Resident" in the Turks & Caicos Islands

After a 3-hour flight, we landed at the Providenciales airport. In addition to the runway, the "airport" had a small bar/cafe at the east end, adjacent to the only road on the island. Although located in this remote part of the Caribbean, the *Provo Airport Cafe* served the best hamburgers, and coldest beer this side of Miami. It was owned by another U. S. ex-patriot, who was also the agent for the only air freight operation in the Turks & Caicos Islands, "Turks Air." All commercial products brought into the country by air were delivered by Turks Air. Anything too large for the freight plane was shipped in by boat and arrived at South Dock at the far south end of the island. One of the benefits of being a "permanent resident" of the T & C is there is no income or sales tax. However, there is a one-time import duty on all "non-perishable goods" brought into the country. Food products, such as milk and eggs, were exempt. This made living on Provo more sustainable, after paying the shipping expense from the U.S.

Transportation from the *Provo Airport* to the Third Turtle Inn was limited. A "permanent resident" most likely would have an old car parked at the airport. It was customary to leave your car parked next to the cafe, often with the keys still in it. The island was sparsely inhabited (total population maybe 100), and everyone knew everyone, locals and "PRs" alike. Crime was almost non-existent, so stealing a car would be pointless, since there was no place to go without getting caught. Occasionally, a car might be "borrowed" for a short trip by a "non-owner", but it was always returned intact, and with the gas tank refilled. In our case, Dupont had a 9 passenger SUV, used to transport guests to and from the hotel to the airport, and out to the beach front lots for sale at Grace Bay. Otherwise, there were 3 island taxis, an odd mix of old, non-air-conditioned junkers, happily rolling along on "may-pop", super-thin tires. As we approached the intersection of the main Provo road, and the even smaller caliche road leading to the hotel. The road sign was labeled "Susie Turn". The sign originated in the early days when a young woman named "Susie" worked at the hotel. Although the side road to the hotel was the only one in the area, Susie would frequently drive past it, and then have to turn around. So, in typical island fashion, Ludington had a road sign posted at the intersection advising - "Susie Turn". The intersection and side road became known as "Susie Turn", and is still there, 60 years later. The road from Susie Turn to the Inn topped a hill where a magnificent view of the ocean prompted first-time visitors to exclaim, "Ooh, what a beautiful view of the ocean ..." ... or ... "Aah, what a magnificent view!" In true island fashion, the hilltop on the road to the Third Turtle Inn became known as "Ooh-Aah Hill".

The Third Turtle Inn was a small, two-story building with the hotel reservation office above, and the kitchen/storeroom on the bottom floor. The restaurant and bar were in an adjacent open-air building. 10 small, one-bedroom cabins, stretched across a small cliff behind the office. The hotel complex was located on the south side of Sellers Pond, a natural harbor for the marina. Dupont showed us the small house adjacent to the guest cabins, which would be our permanent residence. Simple, but clean, and one of the maids cleaned it daily while we were at the hotel. We also had use of the SUV, as needed. I would often make trips to one of the two stores in town for grocery items or other supplies. My wife handled the guest reservation office, while I supervised the bar and maintenance of the grounds, and assisting the boats that came to the marina.

During our time as managers, we had several "celebrity guests" at the hotel. One in particular stands out in my memory. Peter Benchley is the well-known author of the classic novel "Jaws", that had been made into a hit movie in 1975. A fictional story of a giant killer shark terrorizing a small New England coastal community. The movie starred Roy Scheider, Robert Shaw, and Richard Dreyfuss. I recall one morning Benchley came to me and asked if he could take a look at the boats in the marina. I said, "Sure." and accompanied him down to the docks. One particularly nice sailboat was tied alongside one of the walkways. Sitting on the deck was a very attractive young woman in a Bikini, reading. As we approached, we noticed the book was "Jaws". Benchley stepped closer and after saying a polite, "Good Morning", he inquired about the book she was reading. She replied, "It's that new book, "Jaws", about a big shark attacking people near the beach of a small town out east." Whereupon Benchley responded, "How do you like it?" The young girl replied, "Oh, it's OK, but I've read better." Benchley turned to me and laughed, shook his head, and replied, "Oh well. Win some and lose some." I almost collapsed on the dock, laughing. The young girl had a puzzled expression at our laughter, never realizing she had been talking with Peter Benchley, the author of Jaws.

Other celebrities that stayed at the hotel during my stint as manager was Cheryl Crow, and Peter Sellers. And while it was an honor to meet and serve them, nothing significant occurred during their visit. They were just ordinary people, having a good time on their vacation. However, we had one guest that came to fish for marlin with his large offshore boat. He was reputed to be the largest tomato producer in the state of Florida, which along with California, is the largest tomato producing state in the U. S. He and his entourage leased all the guest cabins for 2 weeks. In addition to offshore fishing, he also brought an underwater exploration and salvage crew. Another venture of his was treasure hunting, and he had been successful recently in locating historic ships and sunken treasure off the east coast of the U. S., and the Florida Keys. There had been credible reports from various historical authorities that one of Christopher Columbus' ships, **The Niňa,** had been lost in a hurricane during a subsequent voyage to the new world in the early 1500s in the vicinity of West Caicos. Although **The Niňa** was never located, years later an old ship's anchor was found near West Caicos by an exploration team. Analysis of the anchor reveals that it dates to between 1492 and 1550. The overall size of the anchor and its estimated weight of between 1,200 and 1,500 pounds indicates that it was a "bower" anchor from a 300-ton vessel, the typical size of a Columbus-era ship. The Turks and Caicos discovery is believed to be linked to Vicente Yanez Pinzon - a Spanish sailor, who, along with his brother Martin Alonso Pinzon, was part of the Columbus expeditions.

During the next two years, the Turks & Caicos Islands became a "new discovery" for the tourist industry, and Providenciales was the main attraction. Club Med, the international French resort developer saw the opportunity for a new "destination resort", and contacted Dupont, reserving the entire hotel for a week. Special food and beverages were flown in to accommodate the president and his staff, while they explored Grace Bay for a suitable tract of prime beach-front where the new resort would be built. With the news that Club Med was coming to Providenciales, the island quickly became very popular for tourists and developers wanting to cash in on the "Club Med boom", and therefore necessary for the government to provide an inter-island airline service to accommodate the huge influx of people. At this time, all commercial flights to the Turks and Caicos Islands landed at Grand Turk, the capital, which was 75 miles east of Providenciales. Private air charter was the only means of transportation from the capital to the other islands. And Provo by now, had become the most popular tourist destination in the northwest Caribbean. At the hotel, we were swamped with all types of visitors ... vacationers, honeymooners, real estate investors, and some individuals with "questionable intentions". I remember two in particular.

As the two young men were completing the registration form, with a "tongue in cheek" comment, I said, "Well, I bet you're here to look at real estate." This had become a standing joke around the hotel lately, because everyone was here to "look at property". My comment brought a look of surprise, almost one of alarm. As if I somehow knew the real reason for their visit. With a sheepish smile, they said they were airline pilots from Miami on vacation, and were, in fact, interested in looking at some real estate. Later that evening as they were having drinks in the bar, I mentioned the beach front lots we had for sale a few miles east of the hotel at Grace Bay. They expressed an interest, but never inquired further. For the next few days, they would disappear during the day, and show up later in the evening at the bar. One day, while the maid was cleaning their room, out of curiosity, I looked around their cabin and found a small, handheld walkie-talkie. The same type airline ground personnel use when a plane is either arriving or departing the boarding gates. Not sure what to do at this point, I contacted the local police constable, and told him about finding the radio, and that these guests would disappear every day, and return to the hotel in the late afternoon talking about "the beautiful property they had looked at that day". My question was – how did they know where to look, and who showed it to them? There were no other real estate companies on Provo at this time. I had also noticed on a few occasions that they had not returned to the hotel until the following day. The Provo constable contacted the Chief of Police in Grand Turk, Stanley Williams, advising him of the situation. Chief Williams contacted the DEA and FBI in Miami, advising them of the two pilots and their suspicious activities. As it turned out, the two pilots had been under surveillance by the U.S. authorities as part of a drug smuggling investigation. Although I never learned the outcome, I was fairly certain they would not be flying for a commercial airline anytime soon.

Discovery of the Turks & Caicos Islands as the "new paradise retreat" spread rapidly during the following year, and Providenciales became a "tourist destination" for travel agencies, and vacationers in the United States and Europe. It didn't take long before the British government became aware of the tourism boom and began promoting their remote West Indies possession. One of the first steps was to improve the ability to travel to, from, and around the islands. A decision was made by the British government to establish an island airline service, connecting the individual islands, particularly Grand Turk, the capital of the Turks & Caicos, where the only commercial airline service to the rest of the world was available. Provo became the main focus of this plan, since this was the newly discovered tourist attraction. Opportunists were anxious to take advantage of the new "boom town", and the Third Turtle Inn was the only hotel on Provo.

One of our "special" guests at the hotel was a charming British chap, who had been sent by the British government to establish what was to become the "Turks & Caicos National Airlines". He apparently had extensive experience in establishing airline operations in England, and other parts of Europe. He and Dupont met one evening at the hotel to discuss the government's plan for an inner island airline service. Provo was already the prime destination, and Dupont was a key player in the development of the island. During their discussion, he told Dupont that his first priority was to recruit pilots with experience flying the islands. There were to be 7 locations between Grand Turk at the east end of the island chain, and Providenciales on the west, where small runways were already in place. Three Britain-Norman island airplanes had been purchased and were delivered to Grand Turk by the British government, waiting to be put into service as soon as qualified pilots could be located and checked out. Upon his arrival in Grand Turk, he quickly learned that the island locals were primarily fishermen, and qualified pilots were few and far between. He had hired one young man from Florida, who had been employed to deliver one of the new island planes to Grand Turk. A bush pilot from Canada had also been employed. He needed one more experienced pilot to complete the crew. Dupont, knowing I had considerable island flying experience, asked me to join him and the British airline representative for dinner to discuss the job as a pilot for the new airline. I would still be associated with the hotel, and my wife would handle the day-to-day management of the Inn and restaurant. An agreement was reached, and I became the third and final pilot of the Turks & Caicos National Airlines. Flight schedules called for two planes to depart Grand Turk in the morning going west, making intermediate stops at 6 of the islands, before arriving at Provo around noon. Then reverse the route, arriving back in Grand Turk around 5 in the afternoon. The third plane (assigned to me) was stationed in Provo, and would depart around 7 in the morning, heading east, connecting with the same 6 islands, until reaching Grand Turk around noon. After a lunch break, I would reverse the route, arriving back in Provo around 5 p. m. I flew for the island airline for about a year, before tiring of the monotony of loading passengers, who were usually carrying more baggage than my plane would hold and departing and landing 14 times in a day. When asked about being an "island airline pilot", I would tell people I was nothing more than a "glorified bus driver" - picking up passengers at one location, and dropping them off at the next stop, after only flying a few miles, and never getting more than 300 feet off the ground. It was time to go into business for myself. The islands were becoming more and more populated and private inter island travel was in big demand.

In addition to flying the Turks & Caicos islands, weekly side trips to Haiti became very popular, since the northern city of Cap Haitian was only 100 miles away, with its many tourist shops, and the ancient Citadel fort as the main attractions. So, after leaving the Turks Island Airlines, I decided to start a private charter service based in Providenciales, providing charter service throughout the Turks & Caicos Islands, and to Haiti, and the Bahamas. Being a private charter operation, I was available at whatever time the customer desired, and to locations the island airline didn't serve. At this time there were only two other private charter operations based in Providenciales. Blue Hills Aviation, which was owned and operated by a native Turks islander, Howard Hamilton, and his wife, with whom I would eventually fly for later. The other charter service was "rogue" operator who had come to Providenciales with Fritz Ludington in the early days, mainly hauling freight, and occasionally a few passengers to and from Lantana, Florida.

(Britain-(Norman BN-2 Islander 8 place island airplane)

For my private charter service, I purchased a used Beechcraft Twin Bonanza aircraft – nicknamed "Twin Bo". Years earlier, the trucking company had owned one, and I logged many hours in it. The "Twin Bo" was a large twin engine aircraft, with seating for 6, and ample space for baggage, and was fuel efficient. It wasn't long before the locals realized the comfort and safety of my larger plane, compared to the smaller one available at Blue Hills Aviation. On one occasion I was chartered by the Turks Island police to fly Turks Island police officers to West Caicos on what was supposed to be a drug smuggling interdiction.

The Turks police had received information that a small twin engine plane had landed on the short grass airstrip on West Caicos and was unloading "cargo" onto a small fishing boat tied nearby on the north shore of the island. I flew to West Caicos with three Turks Island Police officers. Two officers, armed with ancient WWII bolt-action rifles, were seated on the floor in the back of the plane, and a lieutenant seated in the co-pilot seat next to me. Flying low, just above the water, and below the view of the smugglers, we approached the north shore of the island. At the precise moment, the plan was to "popped up" over the shoreline at the point where the drug transfer was in process. The rear seats of my plane had been removed, and the two officers were crouched on each side with the plane's rear windows open on each side. The idea was for the officers to shoot out the engines of the smuggler's plane, preventing them from taking off, and then we would land on the runway, and the officers would exit the plane and make the arrests. However, we were in for a real surprise. As the saying goes, "The best laid plans of mice and men …" The smugglers were also armed, but with modern high powered automatic rifles. Upon seeing us approach the runway, they began to fire at us from the ground. Totally caught by surprise, the lieutenant shouted, "Get the Hell out of here!", and I pulled up and away from the runway. The smugglers immediately took off down the runway, climbing out and heading north toward the Bahamas, outrunning my slower plane. Back at West Caicos, the smuggler's boat had fled north, toward the Bahamas at a high rate of speed. I flew back to Grand Turk and dropped off the police officers, and then returned to Provo. After parking the plane, and exiting, I noticed something hanging from the bottom of the fuselage. Upon closer inspection, I saw it was the belly strobe light. It apparently had taken a hit by one of the bullets when the smugglers fired at us. If the bullet had hit a wing, the plane might have either exploded, or caught fire, since that's where the fuel tanks are located. It was definitely a close call.

Living in a "Third World" country back then was certainly different from life in Texas. Out of necessity, the people living there develop unconventional methods for survival. At a first glance, one might think these customs are strange or backwards. Yet, if one thinks about it, they are in reality, very logical. One example of this "problem-solving" process happened when a small group of illegal Jamaican immigrants had been arrested after a weeks-long crime spree. And as luck would have it, I was involved in the drama. One of the unique things I learned after living in the islands for a time was that depending on the country, the local natives will have varying and distinct habits. For example – Haitians will take something that doesn't belong to them. But it is almost always something of minimal value – a jug of water, or a loaf of bread. A necessity of life. In their mind, this isn't really stealing. It's simply a means of survival. On the other hand, Jamaicans have a reputation for being outright thieves. They steal an item for the resale value, or, as in my case, an expensive gold watch for their own personal satisfaction. This episode occurred late one night after we had returned from dinner and had retired. While I was asleep in the next room, the thieves quietly entered the house and discovered a briefcase sitting on the living room sofa. Inside was $250 cash, which I always kept for general purchases at the local store. After taking the money, they very brazenly entered the bedroom where I was asleep and spied the gold watch laying on the nightstand next to the bed. The same Rolex watch mentioned previously in the Matamoros jail episode that had been given to me by my father upon graduation from law school. Needless to say, it was very special. After waking that morning, I discovered the theft. Looking around the house for any clues, I discovered a footprint in some soft sand at the main entry door. It appeared to be the sole of a tennis shoe, and had an unusual, and distinct circular pattern. To preserve the imprint, I placed a small shoe box over it, and immediately went to the local constable's office and reported the theft.

There had been a rash of thefts recently on Provo, and a small group of Jamaicans who had recently arrived, were the prime suspects. A Grand Turk police detective had been sent over to investigate the thefts, and was at the station, and accompanied me back to my house to look around and view the footprint. He brought a Polaroid camera along and snapped a picture of the impression in the sand. I drove him back to the office, where he carefully prepared a bed of soft sand immediately in front of the door. At this time, very few people on the island owned a car, and the constable's office was no exception. The detective needed a car in order to properly investigate the case, so I rented one from a friend who had just opened an auto parts store, and also had a couple of used cars for sale. After a few days, the detective reported that he had located a prime suspect in the island thefts and stealing my watch and cash. He had brought the suspect to his office for questioning. When the suspect entered the constable's office, he stepped onto the soft sand. Sure enough. There it was. The same unique circular footprint that had been left at my house on the night of the theft. After a brief interview, and being shown the footprint evidence, the suspect confessed the string of island thefts and the burglary at my home. He took the investigator to a house where they found the stolen items, including my watch. Unfortunately, by this time, my stolen cash had already been spent. It was indeed very impressive work by a "third world" police investigator.

As I previously mentioned, living in an underdeveloped country, the people must adapt, and develop special ways to survive. It has been said that "Necessity is the Mother of Invention". That was certainly true in my case, and the Turks Island police were no exception. After arresting the thieves, they had to be transported to Grand Turk for official processing, and deportation to Jamaica. My old friend, Chief Williams was contacted, and knowing I had a plane, he asked if I would fly the prisoners and the officers back to Grand Turk. Naturally, I agreed. Unusual for sure, but this is how problems were resolved in the islands. So here we are; me, the victim of the crime, flying my personal airplane to the Turks and Caicos Islands halls of justice, with the thief who stole my watch and money sitting next to me in the co-pilot's seat!

One day Dupont came to the office and told us that an Arab Sheikh, and members of the Saudi royal family would be visiting the island for a week. They had arranged through the family's travel coordinator to rent the entire hotel, all 10 cabins, plus private dining each evening. The coordinator had sent a menu, with a list of the special foods and beverages the family wanted served each at each meal. The entourage, consisting of 10 people, would be arriving in Grand Turk via commercial airline. The Sheikh requested that a private plane large enough to transport him, his family members, and a personal financial advisor meet him at the Grand Turk airport for transportation to Providenciales. I was asked to handle the air travel. The Sheikh was interested in purchasing resort property, and the hotel's eight passenger SUV would be needed to tour the island by road, and a private plane large enough for the Sheikh and his personal financial manager to see the island from the air. The Sheikh's total entourage, in addition to himself, consisted of his Arabic wife, and two teenage sons, his American wife, and small child, a babysitter, the Sheikh's sister, and the Sheikh's personal financial advisor from London. For the next 7 days, the entire hotel and restaurant were closed to the public. One exception was the bar, which the royal family would not need since consumption of alcoholic beverages was prohibited.

During their entire stay, dinner was expected to be served at a specific time. The seating arrangements were that the Sheikh's Arabic wife, two sons, and the sister, would sit by themselves at one dining table, while the Sheikh, his American wife, and the financial advisor would dine at another table. The babysitter and child remained in their hotel room, taking their meals privately. We were also invited each night to dine with the Sheikh at his table. Each day the Sheikh and his advisor toured the island by car and plane, while the rest of the family relaxed at the hotel. After a week, it was time to return the entire group back to Grand Turk. Before departing the hotel, the Arab wife approached my wife and reached for her hand. With only a slight smile, she removed an expensive Sapphire ring from her hand and placed it on my wife's finger. Since she spoke no English, it was a silent statement of gratitude for the personal attention we had paid to her and her family the past week. In Grand Turk before boarding the commercial airliner, the Sheikh handed me his personal solar-powered pocket calculator, and in perfect English, thanked me for the special attention and service we had given him the past week. It had indeed been a very interesting and rewarding experience for everyone involved.

One well-known yachtsman passing through the islands was William Robinson, editor of Yachting, a popular sailing magazine at the time. His travels were subsequently published in the book, "South to The Caribbean". My wife and I were pictured in the book and his stay at our marina was noted as one of the memorable stops on his cruise to the southern Caribbean.

The hotel daily routines returned, with new hotel guests each week, and the resumption of the "Bud & Stud Show" each evening at dinner. During the day, I was either occupied with chartering my sailboat for short trips to neighboring islands or flying day trips to Cap Haitian for "Blue Hills Aviation", a charter service owned by Howard Hamilton, a Turks & Caicos native. On one such trip, I was giving the charter guests a tour of the city. As I was about to cross a street in town, a Haitian standing next to me grabbed my shoulder and pulled me back from the street very abruptly. I turned to the young man who had grabbed my arm, and then back at the street, just as a large Harley Davidson motorcycle sped by. If I hadn't been restrained by the Haitian, I would likely have been run over. As the motorcycle sped off down the road, I thanked the young man, and asked, "Who was that idiot?". He laughed and said, "You were almost run over by Baby Doc!" I replied, "You mean Duvalier, the President of Haiti?" He replied, "Yes. He rides his Harley over here from Port au Prince almost every day, driving through the town at high speeds, running stop lights, and scaring people. But being the President, I guess he can do anything he wants." I thanked him and gave him a dollar (a nice tip in Haiti at the time). Haiti was, and is today, one of the poorest countries in the world. It occupies the western one-third of the island of Hispaniola, sharing with the Dominican Republic, which occupies the other two-thirds to the east. Hispaniola is the second largest island of the West Indies. To its west is Cuba, southwest is Jamaica, and Puerto Rico is to the east. The Bahamas and Turks & Caicos lie to the northwest.

During my years in the Turks & Caicos, I made numerous trips to Cap Haitian and Port au Prince, the capital of Haiti, as well as Puerto Plata, and Samana in the Dominican Republic. After working for Dupont at the hotel for a couple of years, we again decided to move on. Flying, and sailboat charters kept me busy. Although I still had my own plane, I had begun flying part-time for Hamilton at Blue Hills Aviation. He owned two planes. A Piper Aztec, a 4-seat twin, which was used for the short trips, and a Cessna 411, a larger 8 passenger twin used for the longer trips, or when more seating was needed. In the beginning, I mostly flew the Aztec, and Hamilton would do the longer trips in the Cessna. After a few months, Hamilton started taking more time off for his other business at home, and I flew the 411 exclusively on the longer trips to places like the Virgin Islands, the Bahamas, and Florida.

I recall one charter where I was to pick up a single passenger in Great Inagua, Bahamas, and fly him to Port au Prince. Great Inagua is the southernmost island in the Bahamas, a one-hour flight from Provo. The flight from Inagua to Port au Prince is about the same. After landing at the airport in Great Inagua, I went to the customs area searching for a passenger, who had been described as a "tall Anglo dressed in jeans, white shirt, and cowboy boots. Since most people in the remote Bahamas are native Bahamians, the passenger wouldn't be hard to spot. He was over six feet tall, and big enough to play football for the Dallas Cowboys. He saw my cap with the "Blue Hills Aviation" emblem on the front, and captain epaulets on my shirt. He approached saying, "You must be my charter pilot, I'm John Smith." We shook hands, and I thought to myself, "Hmm... John Smith... Really?" When we reached the plane, I asked if he had any luggage. He replied that he only had the small attaché case he was carrying. Boarding the plane, I asked if I could place the attaché case in the baggage compartment. He replied, "Thank you. I prefer to keep it with me.". "John Smith" had just sent a signal that this charter was not what it appeared.

We departed Great Inagua and climbed to our planned cruising altitude for the one-hour flight to Port au Prince. About halfway across Turks Passage, a 100 mile-wide, open body of water separating the Bahamas and Haiti. Sitting next to me in the co-pilot seat, he asked, "Have you flown from the Bahamas to Haiti many times?" When I replied that I had, he asked, "Will the Haiti customs people check the passport I used in Great Inagua?" Startled, I replied, "That's the normal process in my experience. Why do you ask?" He replied, "I didn't plan to use the same passport at Port au Prince." I almost fainted. Rapidly collecting my thoughts, I replied, "Well, I've never seen that done, but I guess you can try it and see." From that point on, we had no further conversation for the rest of the flight. My mind was rushing with thoughts about what this guy was up to. What was in the attaché case? A gun? Counterfeit money? Drugs? If he is searched at Haitian Customs, and they find contraband, or a weapon, what will happen to me and the plane? The Matamoros nightmare from years before vividly flashed through my mind.

Upon landing at the Port au Prince airport, I taxied to the Customs & Immigration area, with thoughts of what would happen next racing through my mind. What would Haitian Immigration do when they saw the name on "John Smith's" passport was not the name he used when departing Great Inagua? Again, the Matamoros nightmare returned. Only this time, even worse. This airplane didn't belong to me. Fortunately, we were greeted by an immigration official I had dealt with on my previous trips to Port au Prince. I quickly told him I had another charter waiting and needed to return to Provo as soon as possible. He smiled, and waived me back to my plane, where I quickly called the tower for an immediate takeoff back to Provo. Another bullet dodged! Back in Provo, I called Hamilton and told him what happened. He laughed and said, "I guess from now on, my wife needs to check our prospective customers a bit closer." I managed to smile, and agreed, still having thoughts of what could have been another "Matamoros Nightmare", two thousand miles from home.

By now, between working at the Inn, and my flying, we had managed to save enough money to buy a piece of property and build a home. We had been renting a small home just east of the hotel, overlooking the entrance to Seller's Pond. The location was high on a ridge and afforded an excellent position for me to assist new arrivals with navigating the tricky entrance channel. I became very adept at guiding boats safely inside the reef even at night, communicating with the captain via VHF radio, using a stopwatch, and flashlights, I would advise him when to turn at the precise moment. In time, I became known as the person to contact when approaching Provo in a boat for the first time. I was even mentioned in the "Yachtsman's Guide To The Bahamas", a very popular sailor's guide when traveling in the Bahamas, and neighboring Turks & Caicos Islands. At this time there were no telephones on the island. The only means of communication between residents, as well as boats, was by marine (VHF) radio. Everyone monitored VHF channel 13, and everyone had a "handle". Mine was "Honeysuckle", named for my boat. Howard Hamilton's wife used "Blue Hills" when she would call me to fly a charter. Other local "handles" were "Pine Cay", a neighboring island whose only occupants were the managers of a small tourist resort, "Third Turtle" (our hotel), "Turks Air", our only air freight operation, "South Dock", and "Leeward", (Leeward Going Through), a small hotel and restaurant at the eastern end of Providenciales. Life was good. Very simple by most standards, but very good, nevertheless. If you were fortunate enough to own a car, you were very popular. Gas was $2.50 a gallon, even back then. However, the furthermost point was only ten miles away. And the roads were such that speeds were necessarily limited to less than 30 mph. A tank of gas would last for several weeks, even months. At home, water was stored in cisterns, purchased from the only water truck that retrieved it from a local well for delivery, or, alternatively, collecting rainwater from a roof collecting system, which drained into our cistern. It was then supplied to the house by hand, or with an electric pump. The electric pumps at first were battery-powered, but later with a modern electric pump, if you owned a portable generator.

For lighting, we used kerosene lanterns, or candles. Cooking and refrigeration were done with either propane or kerosene stoves, and refrigerators. A propane refrigerator ran for weeks at a time before needing a refill. Using a kerosene stove or refrigerator required weekly refills. In time, the island began to switch to small portable AC generators. This was a definite improvement over kerosene or propane, but still required storing the fuel. We had to draw water from the cistern in the evening before going to bed, in the we needed a drink of water, or flush a toilet later in the night. There was no television on the island at this time. It would come later, however. "Simmons Store" was originally owned by one of the early island "ex-patriots", that arrived shortly after Fritz Ludington built the Third Turtle Inn.

It stocked most of the basic foods and household items needed – bread, milk, eggs, canned goods, etc. It was located conveniently in the center of town, and across the road from a grocery and dry goods store, which was owned by an island local. Simmons sold out shortly after we arrived to an American looking to capitalize on the popularity boom of Providenciales. He became instantly unpopular with the locals and ex patriots, alike, and lasted only a couple of years, before selling out to a Canadian company that had recently arrived on the island and had begun developing the old "downtown" district. Third Turtle marina manager, Doc Withey, having been one of the early U.S. settlers, quickly seized the opportunity and opened "Carib West", the only liquor store on the island. And since Withey and Dupont were close friends, the Third Turtle Inn naturally purchased all of its alcoholic products from Carib West, as did everyone else. Carib West was located in a small retail complex Withy had opened shortly after arriving on the island.

("Hud'n Hud'n" – a stripped-down Citroen with 2-cylinder air-cooled engine.
Brian and T-Bone (seated left) in my driveway. Notice red gas "tank" behind Whatley)

Ludington recruited a south Florida native for the purpose of opening a scuba diving operation at the hotel. He had been a lifeguard and experienced scuba diver from Delray Beach. Ludington offered him the exclusive scuba dive operation for the hotel. "Provo Turtle Divers" was situated in a small cave located near the hotel. The operation began with one open lifeboat, Provo Turtle Divers offered diving and snorkeling trips to view the brilliant-colored tropical fish, and reefs along the coast and bay just outside Seller's Pond. Shortly thereafter, a glass-bottom boat was added for underwater sightseeing the reefs and marine life from above. Years later, Provo Turtle Divers added an offshore fishing yacht for charter, taking the serious fisherman offshore in search of marlin and sword fish. As the island began to grow, the business community developed also. New shops and services began to spring up. Flying daily to and from the other islands, especially Grand Turk, I met and became close friends with most of the government officials, and business owners, most of whom were charter customers. One particularly interesting gentleman was a British Army colonel who had moved to the islands after retiring from service. He had lived on Grand Turk for many years and published a local weekly newspaper called the "Turks Island Weekly". He would jokingly refer to it as the *"Turks Island Weakly"*. The colonel and I became good friends. Most days my charter flights included a stop at Grand Turk for lunch. At the time the Turks Head Inn was the only hotel on Grand Turk, with a popular bar and restaurant where the local business establishment gathered daily. I would always find the colonel sitting at the bar with his ever-present glass of Scotch whiskey, reliving stories from his military past, and complaining about an unpopular (at least in his mind) government official. The colonel was instrumental in organizing the first Turks Island Chamber of Commerce, and he asked me to serve as the Providenciales representative. One very prominent member of the Chamber of Commerce was a young Turks Islander named Washington Misick, who owned a real estate company – "Prestigious Properties". He had just opened an office on Provo and asked my wife and I to be his designated agents. Misick was very personable and intelligent, and later became Chief Minister of the Turks & Caicos Islands, with the same power and prestige as the President of the U.S. Thirty-five years later, after leaving Providenciales and returning to Texas, my friend Washington Misick would enter my life again ... in a most unbelievable way.

21

CHAPTER

Conch Fritters and Country Music

Who, other than a Texan, would dare open a country-western saloon in the Caribbean? The idea of a country-western bar came about after leaving the Third Turtle Inn. We became aware how the island was growing as a result of the French corporation, Club Med, decision to open a resort at Grace Bay. One requirement before the resort could open was the construction of an airport that would accommodate commercial passenger aircraft. A major international construction company, Johnson Construction, Ltd., was hired by the British government to replace the old dirt airstrip with a large, all-weather runway, including proper lighting, and aircraft communication equipment, and also widen and pave the main road leading from the airport to Grace Bay. This construction process brought in many workers and their families for the next two years. I invited my old "Breaker Corporation" friend to come for a visit. He and his wife flew to Provo, and we discussed my idea of opening an authentic Texas saloon. They thought it was a great idea, especially considering the fact that the island population was growing fast with the arrival of the British construction workers. Another local resident who had been a regular patron at the Third Turtle bar, and was a licensed architect, was hired to design the building. He came up with one that resembled an old Texas barn, with full-width porch, and open windows that were closed and locked after closing each night. At the top of "Ooh-Aah Hill", on the same road from "Susie Turn" to the Third Turtle Inn, we purchased property large enough to accommodate the building, and plenty of parking, and with a grand view of the ocean. No air conditioning was needed, as the weather in these islands remained very mild most of the year. We built a bar that ran almost the entire length of the building, capable of seating twenty or more at a time, with small tables scattered throughout the

73

open room, and an area reserved for dancing. My father had passed away a year earlier, and we had sold the ranch located in Tioga, Texas, where Mom had lived for the past several years. Tioga is about 35 miles from Dallas, and Mom wanted to be closer to her brother and sister-in-law, and other family members. So, she and her housekeeper moved to a home in north Dallas. Dad had several pictures of the ranch and his horses hanging on the walls in the living room, and hallways. These were packed up and stored at the trucking company after Mom moved back to Dallas. I contacted the office manager at the trucking company and made arrangements to have several pictures shipped to Provo, and hung them on the walls of the Saloon, as a tribute to my father and the Bar BH Ranch. One of our regular patrons at the Saloon was a distant relative of the British royal family and owned a vacation home on Provo. He carried the formal British title of "Earl", but was in reality, very down-to-earth and a talented artist. Using a small pen knife, he etched a drawing of my mother on her horse into the wooden bar top. Carving initials into the bar top became a popular pastime with the patrons, while enjoying a cool beverage.

Another addition to the bar, which was added to attract the British construction workers, was two genuine English dart boards, complete with a chalk scoreboards, laid out exactly as they were in England. This proved to be very popular, not only for the Brits, but the locals as well. Soon, dart tournaments became the rage, and we offered prize money for the winners. With the dart games in progress and bar patrons having their favorite beverages, Willie Nelson, and Waylon Jennings singing "On The Road Again" in the background, we were packed every evening. The *Bar BH Saloon* name was suggested by my Dallas friend's wife, in honor of my late father, and quickly became the most popular drinking establishment on the island. Fortunately, the English government didn't have maximum occupancy rules for bars at the time, because most nights, especially weekends, we would have over 100 people inside the bar, as well as out on the grand porch overlooking the ocean. And I was aware how the British love their "pints". Since the other restaurants and bars mostly sold refrigerated American beer, I catered to the British construction group, by serving their beer "English-style", at room temperature. No other bar on the island served beer at room temperature. As a result, more than twenty construction workers became regular Bar BH customers. However, one unfortunate incident happened while I was away from the bar on an overnight trip. I had left my son, Kerry, in charge of the bar. He had been a part-time bar manager in Dallas and was staying with us for the summer. After closing the bar one evening, Kerry found one of our regulars, a purported "real estate investor" from Canada, slumped over in his vehicle in the parking lot with bullet hole in his head. The island police were called. As a result of their investigation, the police learned the victim was involved in drug trafficking on the island and apparently had crossed another local dealer.

An unexpected bonus of the saloon's popularity was local interest in cowboy shirts and jeans. The native islanders who normally favored island-style "reggae" music, became attracted to Willie Nelson, Waylon Jennings, and Merle Haggard music, jeans and boots. My wife's small island shop, "Conch's Closet", was swamped with requests for cowboy hats, jeans, and western shirts. She and her partner had to relocate to a larger space to accommodate the increased business. During the flurry of interest in the country western scene, I was contacted by a writer for the National Inquirer and interviewed for an article. When it came out it featured a picture of me in my pilot uniform and a cowboy hat, straddling an engine on the plane like I was riding a bucking bronc with one hand high in the air. The caption read: *"Texas businessman leaves a $100,000/year job and opens a country-western saloon in the islands."* The story was also published in the Austin-Statesman American newspaper in Austin, Texas. I was later told the **Bar BH Saloon** was the only country-western bar in the entire Caribbean at the time. The Bar BH Saloon became a popular spot not only for tourist from the hotels, but also boaters passing through to the southern Caribbean islands.

Three years after opening the Bar BH, working from early morning to late at night, we finally "burned out". It was time for a slower pace. A regular customer from Canada interested in investment opportunities on the island, approached me with an offer to purchase the saloon. We agreed on a price, and I sold the Bar BH Saloon. Not being a cowboy or country western music fan, he changed the theme of the bar back to island décor and music. I returned to full-time charter flying and helping out at "Conch's Closet. One of the new companies that had arrived on Provo was Caicos Petroleum. They were involved in the logistics of transferring fuel from large super tankers that weren't able to enter many of the shipping terminals due to their size and draft, onto smaller vessels that could. "Lightering", as it was called, became very popular and the relatively calm waters just off the coast of West Caicos provided the ideal location for positioning to two large vessels close enough to pass a large hose across and pump the fuel from the larger ship to the smaller one. Caicos Petroleum stationed an 80-foot utility vessel at South Dock, which was used to handle passing the transfer hose between the two large tankers. The manager of the company frequently needed an airplane for transportation to and from their mainland office in Florida and for observing the transfer operations off West Caicos. Having both an airplane, and local knowledge of the islands, I was hired to handle the air transportation needs, as well as serve as caretaker of the 80-foot lightering boat. On one occasion during the tropical storm season, it was decided that the boat should be re-located to a safer anchorage until after the predicted arrival of a tropical storm had passed. With two friends as crew, I moved the 80-foot boat from South Dock around the north end of Provo, and into Seller's Pond without incidence for safe keeping. It remains the largest boat I have ever captained. Eventually, as larger shipping ports were built, lightering fuel became unnecessary, and Caicos Petroleum closed its Provo operation, and I sold my airplane to Caicos Petroleum where the local manager used it for trips to Florida.

By now the islands were attracting a multitude of investors and the quiet, laid-back lifestyle of Providenciales rapidly began to change. The political party that previously had been friendly to foreigners living in the islands lost the majority in the legislature. The opposing party that took control of the government was not as friendly toward foreigners as the previous regime, implementing strict rules and regulations for non-native residents. A permanent resident certificate (PRC) became harder to get and renew. I began to have fears that we may soon find it hard to own a business on Provo without having to take in a native partner. Recently, a couple of my former Texas sailing friends had arrived in Provo on their boats. During our conversations about how things were back in Texas, they mentioned that the south Texas coast was still a nice laid-back place to live. A major factor in my decision to move back home was since my father had passed away, Mom was living alone with only her live-in housekeeper as a companion. I needed to be closer to Mom. I decided to move back to Texas, but I really wasn't ready for the big city atmosphere, and cold winters of Dallas. My Texas sailing friends had convinced us that the south Texas coast was where we should be. It would be closer to Mom and easier to stay in touch via telephone, or visits by car. Port Isabel on the south Texas coast, was a good compromise for boating and year-round temperate weather. I flew to South Texas on an "exploratory trip" and began searching for a suitable home in the Port Isabel/South Padre area. Ironically, a former acquaintance from my earlier days at Rancho Viejo was now living on South Padre Island and had a real estate agent friend there. Ironically, I had met them previously when they came to Providenciales on vacation. The agent showed me several residential properties on South Padre and Port Isabel, and I ultimately bought a condo in Port Isabel with a marina and access to the Laguna Madre Bay and the Gulf of Mexico.

Meanwhile back on Provo, the Canadian company that owned the shopping center where Conch's Closet was located bought the store, and we said goodbye to our former partner at the Conch's Closet, our diver friend at Provo Turtle Divers, and the owner of Blue Hills Aviation. With mixed emotions and sadness, we loaded our personal belongings in a shipping container, listed our home with Washington Misick at Prestigious Properties, and flew back to Texas. This was April 1984. We had lived in the Turks & Caicos Islands for almost 6 years. Two years after leaving Provo, a fierce tropical storm hit the island, destroying many homes. Our former home was one that was leveled. Our former partner sent us a picture showing nothing standing except our refrigerator on an otherwise bare foundation. It was a sad to see our house gone, but thankful we were not there when the storm hit.

22

CHAPTER

The Last Hurrah

The first three years back in Texas I became involved in the boating and social activities at the Laguna Madre Yacht Club, a small group of sailing enthusiasts in Port Isabel. They had a small clubhouse near the marina in Port Isabel where we socialized and had sailboat races and short cruises in the area. After a year or so my wife became bored, and decided to open another store, similar to the one on Providenciales. She particularly wanted to be on South Padre Island with its larger number of affluent tourists. She found an ideal location at "Saida Plaza", a new retail center just across the Queen Isabella Causeway from Port Isabel. She asked her sister in Dallas to join her in the new venture. They named it "Sisters Trading Company". It became an instant success. Years later, they moved to a larger facility, focusing on interior design, changing the name to "Sisters Interiors". Forty years later, it remains one of the most popular interior design shops in South Texas. Three years after moving to Port Isabel, I became acquainted with an older gentleman who had a home for sale on South Padre Island. We became friends through our mutual interest in golf. He lived in Harlingen and wasn't using his home on the island, and offered it to me at fair price, and even agreed to finance it. It was ideally situated on one of the boat canals and had a perfect dock for my sailboat, so we sold the condo and moved to South Padre Island. I continued my sailing activities, while my wife and her sister became absorbed with the store. And falling back on my earlier days as owner of the biggest saloon in the Caribbean, I opened an island liquor store called "Padre Spirits". In addition to having a retail package store, I was also licensed to sell alcoholic beverage products to the local bars and restaurants. At the time there were 22 licensed bars or restaurants that offered alcoholic beverages. My main competition in this "club business" was Feldman's. A large family-owned corporation, they had been on the island for several years, and had over 20 retail stores across the Rio Grande Valley. At the suggestion of the food and beverage manager of the island's Hilton Hotel, I decided to get into the club business, selling alcoholic beverages wholesale to the bars, restaurants, and hotels. The Hilton Hotel was my first customer, and ironically, the hotel's beverage manager, who had initially convinced me to enter the club business, was the ex-husband of my future wife, Sandra – *small world!* In less than one year after getting into the very competitive "club business", I had secured 21 of the 22 licensed establishments on South Padre Island as regular customers. I accomplished this by giving personal service to each customer – large or small. A lesson I learned from my father. No small feat for an individual taking on the largest liquor store operator in the region. I call it "My David and Goliath Moment"! It wasn't long before I received a phone call from the owner of Feldman Liquors, inviting me to have lunch at the Harlingen Country Club. I accepted and I was pretty sure why he called. At lunch, he told me how impressed he was with my ability to take most of his island club business. However, he said he knew neither of us were making a profit because of the low prices we were forced into selling the liquor to the clubs, primarily because of our intense competition. He proposed a "truce". He offered to buy me out and have me work for him overseeing the island stores and club business. I thank him for the lunch and the offer, but I needed to think about his offer and get back to him.

Before I could get back to Feldman with an answer, a "new horse" entered the race. A wealthy Mexican businessman who lived in McAllen, had opened up a package store in Edinburg, a town located about 70 miles west of South Padre Island. He was planning on expanding his retail package stores to South Padre Island and was interested in buying my retail store. Again, I was invited to lunch and while we were seated at the restaurant, he pushed a paper sack that was under the table toward me and motioned for me to open it. When I opened it I saw it was jam full of bank-wrapped $100 bills. $15,000 cash. $5000 more than I had initially invested when I opened "Padre Spirits" only a couple of years earlier. He wanted no "paper trail", so there was no paperwork to sign. And I think I know why! All we had to do was change the name on the store's lease contract, changing it into his corporation's name. The deal was concluded in less than an hour. Now my problem was how to deposit $15,000 without raising a "red flag" with the IRS. The president of my local bank on South Padre Island had the solution. I deposited $7,500 into my account on one day, and a couple days later, I made another $7,500 deposit. This effectively and legally avoided the IRS "red flag" rule requiring banks to "red flag" an account (meaning – notify the IRS) if a $10,000, or more deposit is made at any given time. I was getting tired of the late hours in order to keep patronizing my club customers, and the retail package store business was boring. And working for Feldman's didn't appeal to me. I had been setting my own pace for too many years now to return to punching a time clock. Again – It was time for me to move on.

(A "raft-up" in Laguna Madre Bay, Port Isabel, Texas)

One evening I received a call from the mayor of South Padre asking if we could meet at a local restaurant. Knowing I was an attorney, he asked if I would be interested in serving as the municipal judge of SPI. The current judge was apparently involved in an embarrassing situation with a lady at a local bar and had to resign. The municipal judge position is appointed by the mayor, as opposed to being elected. I accepted the appointment and was sworn in as the presiding judge of South Padre in 1988 and served the town for 8 years. The island at this time was peaceful and quiet. Traffic tickets and "drunk and disorderly" arrests were the primary offense, particularly during Spring Break when the influx of college students who stormed the island resulted in many humorous moments, too numerous to detail here. However, a couple stand as memorable. One incident during Spring Break, the island police arrested a young reveler, who had jumped into a parked police cruiser thinking it was an island taxi, and in a slurred, inebriated voice exclaimed, "Take me to the Radisson!" (one of the more popular hotels on the beach). The officer replied, "You got it.", and promptly transported him to the municipal jail. When he was brought before me the next morning, I carefully explained the difference between an "island taxi", and a "police cruiser". He timidly replied, "I guess I was a little too drunk to tell the difference, Your Honor." The entire courtroom broke out in laughter.

A very memorable incident happened as result of being the island judge; I met my future wife, Sandra, for the first time. She was manager and a part-owner of a very popular bar called, "The Island Pub". It was the favorite drinking establishment for the late-night crowd, attracting its biggest crowds between the hours of 10 p.m. to 2 a.m. The octagonal shaped building in the center of town had previously been a bar named "The Officers Club", an early afternoon happy hour favorite of the older generation. The interior walls were covered with old military pictures and memorabilia by the previous owner. Sandra and her partners bought the building and transformed it into a late-night disco, complete with a DJ, a dance floor, and fast service. It quickly became the most popular late-night bar, having more than its share of loud music and rowdy patrons, which resulted in frequent police intervention. During one particular Spring Break, after the police had received numerous calls complaining about the late-night noise, I asked the police to have the manager appear in court. Sandra ("Sandy") Wright appeared in court the next day and I explained the problem with the numerous complaints about the loud noise and fights. She agreed to be more vigilant removing persons that caused a disturbance. Shortly thereafter, the noise and fights subsided to an acceptable level. I thanked her for her cooperation, and not very long after this meeting I asked her to dinner. This is when I learned that she was the ex-wife of the Hilton beverage manager that had convinced me to get into the "club liquor business" earlier. Eventually, we began dating and were married a couple of years later. In November 2023, Sandy and I celebrated our 25th anniversary.

(Sandra Hunsaker)

As a sitting municipal court judge, another duty was serving as a "magistrate" for the local county precinct. One responsibility involved holding an "inquest" to determine if the person died from other than natural causes such as an intentional act (murder or suicide), an accident, or other unusual circumstances. In one such case I was called when the police found a partially submerged truck in the shallow waters of the Laguna Madre. Inside the cab was the body of a man with a bullet hole in his head. Since no weapon was found in the truck, it was determined that the man had been shot and the truck pushed into the bay. When the tide ebbed out, the top of the truck surfaced, revealing the body inside. After investigation by the local police and the Cameron County Drug Task Force, it was determined that the victim had been murdered as a result of a drug deal that had gone bad.

A few years later I moved from the island to Bayview, a small "bedroom community", where I was appointed city attorney. In addition, I had also joined a local law firm in Brownsville, handling mostly criminal and divorce cases. As an aside, during my many years in the practice of law, I have come to the conclusion that divorce and child custody cases are by far the most unpleasant to handle. And there's a logical reason why. In other areas of the law practice, one of the participants almost always walks out of the courtroom satisfied and happy – a plaintiff with a large settlement in a personal injury case, a "not guilty" verdict in a criminal case, or a prosecutor who wins a guilty verdict and a long prison sentence for a habitual criminal. In a divorce or child custody case, both parties are mad at the other because neither side gets everything they expected. In my many years of practice, I have never had a divorce client walk out of the courtroom with a big smile on their face.

In 1995, I was contacted by the city manager of Los Fresnos, Texas, a somewhat larger town about 10 miles from Bayview, offering me the job as City Attorney. I accepted and moved my law office from Brownsville to Los Fresnos, renting a small building that had been a veterinary clinic. Los Fresnos is on State Highway 100, halfway between South Padre Island and U.S. 83/77, the main highway from Harlingen to Brownsville, not far from my previous home at Rancho Viejo, and the primary route to the island. Los Fresnos had gained the dubious reputation of being a "speed trap" city from an article published in the popular magazine "Texas Monthly". The quickest route for vacationers and spring breakers in a hurry to get to the island was State Highway 100 directly through Los Fresnos. The municipal court docket was constantly crowded with speeding violations. After being in office a few months, I found out that there was an "unwritten policy" to issue a speeding ticket for speeds over 4 miles above the 30-mph posted speed limit. I felt this was a little too strict, since Highway 100 was a 4-lane highway passing through the commercial district of the town with a red light at a main intersection in the middle of town controlling the flow of traffic. In time, I prevailed on the city council and a new "unwritten directive" was instituted making 10 miles over the posted speed limit the standard for issuing a citation. Coincidentally, one of the long-time residents of Los Fresnos was an ex-Army buddy of Elvis Presley and held an open celebration each year on Elvis' birthday. He and I reminisced about our memories of meeting the "King of Rock and Roll". After serving 6 years as City Attorney, I was contacted by the City of Harlingen, offering me the job as a municipal court judge after the previous long-time judge had retired. Sandra and I had previously moved from the small Bayview home to a larger house in San Benito, Texas situated halfway between Los Fresnos, and Harlingen. My neighbor and friend in San Benito was the Justice of Peace for the San Benito precinct, and he asked if I would be interested in being municipal judge in San Benito. I accepted this appointment also, and now had the unique distinction of being municipal judge simultaneously in adjoining municipalities, whose city limit signs were mounted on the same post!

Although most of the time municipal judge duties are not exciting or dangerous, traffic court is usually dull and boring, so dozing off in traffic court is not unusual. However, municipal judges are also by state law a magistrate judge with the responsibility of arraigning defendants charged with serious misdemeanors or felonies, and to set their bail. A person charged with a serious crime is different than someone who received a traffic citation and can often result in threats to the judge, requiring twenty-four-hour police protection, as I was about to learn. One day I received a phone call from a lawyer who had previously rented office space from me in Los Fresnos and had relocated to McAllen. He immediately inquired if I was "OK". Puzzled at his question, I assured him that I was fine and asked why he was so concerned. He said one of his clients had told him that he heard there was a "contract out on Judge Hunsaker" apparently by an unhappy defendant I had previously arraigned. My lawyer friend said he wasn't sure if it was true, but he had called the FBI anyway, and wanted me to know. It wasn't long before I received a call from the FBI advising me of the threat, and if I had any idea who it might be. I told the agent I had no idea, and that it could be anyone of many who had appeared in my court. The FBI notified the San Benito and Harlingen police departments of the threat, and they each assigned a patrol car to watch my house and follow my wife and me whenever we left the house. A Harlingen PD officer stayed with my wife if I had to leave, and she would often prepare lunch for him. He also would answer our phone and inquire who was calling. This routine went on for a couple of months, but investigators were never able to determine who had made the threat. After a few weeks without further threats the twenty-four-hour protection ended.

After living in San Benito for five years, we found that we were spending more time in the Harlingen area shopping and socializing with new friends. We both had wanted to build our own home, so we purchased a nice residential lot and hired a building contractor. Eight months later we moved into our new home in a nice neighborhood on the west side of Harlingen. One day, while the home was still under construction, a Cameron County Drug Task Force investigator, and long-time Harlingen police detective, called and asked if I was available to issue a search warrant. He explained that his task force team had located a group of local drug dealers hold up in a mobile home park not far from my house. He wanted to search the premises and arrest the occupants before they could move to another location. I told him I was at my new house and to come by and I would issue the warrants. After signing the warrants, I ask him if he would like to come in and take a look at the house. He declined, saying he would take a rain check and needed to get back to the trailer park and execute the warrants before the suspects took off. After he left, I went back inside the house to see how the work was progressing. Once inside I noticed the distinctive aroma of marijuana. When I entered the room where the tile crew had been laying floor tile, I found them taking a break laughing while passing around a marijuana joint! A few days later, I ran into the investigator and told him what he had missed by not coming in to see my house. We both had big laugh, and still today we both have a good laugh reliving this humorous, "close call" incident.

I had joined the Harlingen Elks Lodge earlier in 1998 and it had become the focus of our social activity. One particular member of the lodge who would eventually become one of my best friends was Dr. John Boling. I had met John previously in Los Fresnos while representing a local farmer in a crop insurance claim. Dr. Boling had a PhD from Texas A&M in entomology, the science of crop diseases and parasites.

He was known state-wide as the foremost expert in this field and was employed by numerous insurance companies and farmers with insurance claims and crop issues. A longtime member of the Harlingen Elks Lodge and chairman the lodge house committee, Boling called one day and asked if I would join his committee. The house committee is the governing body for the lodge social quarters, which includes the bar and restaurant, and entertainment for the weekly dances. Eventually I was given the responsibility of booking the various bands that played at the lodge weekly. John and I remained close friends until his passing in September 2022. His wife asked me to give the eulogy at John's funeral. The agricultural community had lost an icon, and I had lost a very special friend.

As a result of my work on the house committee the the current Exalted Ruler (a fancy name for "president") asked me to serve as the Lodge Esquire, a position similar to a "sergeant at arms", keeping order and decorum in the lodge room during meetings and escorting new candidates around the lodge, while reciting specific dialogue for the initiation of new members. I've had a good memory since childhood and could quickly memorize the lyrics of a song or verses of poetry. By the end of my first year as the Lodge Esquire I had become very proficient in the Esquire dialogue and movements. However, I would be remiss if I did not give full credit to Ted Brookshire who spent several hours a week working with me perfecting my dialogue delivery and movements. The Harlingen Elk Lodge ritual team became well known in the Elk South District, which consisted of seven lodges - Kingsville on the north, McAllen and Laredo on the west, Brownsville and San Benito on the south, and Harlingen, and Weslaco in the center of the district. We were frequently asked to perform initiation ritual ceremonies at the other area lodges. At one state convention our Harlingen ritual team placed second behind the Houston lodge in the state-wide ritual competition.

Perhaps the most popular lodge custom is the reciting of "Eleven O'clock Toast" by a lodge member at 11:00 each evening when lodge members are present. And every year the Texas State Elk Association at its annual convention they have an "Eleven O'clock Toast" competition. Contestants from each lodge are invited to participate and are judged by a five-member statewide panel of ritual instructors and former winners of the competition. I had been elected Exalted Ruler of the Harlingen Elks Lodge in 2005 and attended the annual convention that year. At dinner the first night, Brookshire said he wanted me to sign up for the competition. I was reluctant at first, but he insisted. The competition is held in a private room with only the five judges and the contestants present. When I entered the room I was startled to see Ted Brookshire sitting at the judges table. After collecting myself, I did my presentation of the Eleven O'clock Toast and returned to my hotel room to await the results that would be announced at dinner later that evening. While seated at the dinner table with Ted and other Harlingen lodge members, I noticed Ted was smiling when he complimented me on my earlier performance. After the dinner, I was ready to leave before the award presentations certain I had not won, but Ted insisted I stay. Apparently, he knew something I didn't. When my name was announced as the winner of the Eleven O'clock Toast I almost fell out of my chair! This is the proudest moment in my 26 years as a member of the Elks organization, even surpassing my previous election as Exalted Ruler. A humorous anecdote occurred when I was told my score was 99 out of a possible 100. This meant one of the judges had given me less than a perfect score on his card. I asked Ted if he could tell me which judge it was. He grinned and replied, "It was me. You mispronounced a 'the' in the dialogue recitation." *Explanation:*

In the Benevolent and Protective Order of Elks ritual, depending on its usage in a sentence, the word "the" is sometimes pronounced "thuh", instead of "thee". Up to this point we had all been surprised that Ted was going to be involved in my competition, since he was from our lodge, and my personal tutor. It is no wonder that Ted Brookshire was known state-wide as "Mr. Elk". He was a man of extremely high morals and integrity, and a very special friend in my life. Sadly, Ted passed away a few years later.

About this time a couple of friends had taken up "cruising" on motorcycles. So not to be outdone, I had to give it a try. Sandy is originally from the "Harley Davidson Capitol of the World" - Wisconsin. She politely told me if I insisted on buying a motorcycle it better be a Harley. Sandy and I went to the local Harley dealership and looked at several models. Not knowing the first thing about motorcycles, I asked one of the salesmen to show me something that a beginner would be able to handle. The salesman was an experienced biker and knew the Harley Davidson line very well. He showed us several and I ultimately purchased a cruising model that would seat two persons and two saddlebags for luggage. For the next few years, cruising on our Harley with biker friends took the place of planes and boats. The new Harley Davidson dealership was forming a Harley Owners Group (HOG) at that time and asked me to serve as its first president. In a short period, I had gone from knowing practically nothing about motorcycles to the prestigious position of being Director of the first Harley Davidson Owners Group in South Texas.

One of my local friends, Mike Heckman, was the president of our local motorcycle club, "Spartan Cruisers". Mike also has a very interesting past. Born and raised in Germany, until his family moved to the states when he was fourteen. At the time, Mike did not speak a word of English. However, by the time he graduated from high school, he could speak perfect English without a trace of an accent. After becoming a U. S. citizen, Mike joined the U.S. Air Force and honorably served his adopted country for twenty years. But he wasn't done yet. Upon retiring from the Air Force, Mike joined the U. S. Customs & Immigration Service as the lead bus mechanic at the Bayview, Texas detention center, where he remained for another twenty years, having served his adopted country for 40 years. A remarkable accomplishment for someone who came to the United States as an immigrant! Mike and I, along with other members of the Spartan Cruisers, cruised south Texas. Each summer we would ride to Missouri touring Lake of the Ozarks and other interesting areas in Missouri. One interesting ride took us to Whiteman Air Force Base in Knob Noster, MO. Whiteman is the home base for the B-52 "Spirit" stealth bomber. At times the Air Force will allow visitors on the base, and on this particular occasion we were allowed to ride our bikes into Whiteman Air Base. After entering the facility, we learned that country and western recording artist, Lee Greenwood, would be performing a live concert on an outside stage that had been set up near the main runway of the airfield. Greenwood was onstage facing the large crowd with is back to the runway. As he was singing his super hit, "Proud to Be An American", a B-52 stealth bomber had landed and was taxiing to the parking ramp, immediately behind the stage. The crowd began to cheer loudly as the pilot taxied the giant aircraft close up behind Greenwood. Oblivious to the approaching bomber, Greenwood assumed the applause and wild cheering was for his hit song. He smiled and acknowledged the applause and continues singing, while the crowd frantically kept pointing for him to turn around. With the very imposing bomber only a few feet from the stage,

Greenwood finally turned around and stopped singing and joined the rest of the crowd, waiving to the B-52's crew. It was certainly a "Kodak Moment".

(The B-52 Spirit stealth bomber

By now we had bought a summer home in Warsaw, and each spring would drive to Warsaw, towing the bike behind in a trailer. On one ride to Eureka Springs, Arkansas, we had a minor accident at a restaurant parking lot laying the bike over, resulting in Sandy breaking a small bone in her wrist. After seeing a local physician, she was advised not to ride on the bike back to Warsaw. Fortunately, another close friend and fellow biker had a large bike trailer. I called him and advised him of our predicament, whereupon he immediately came to Eureka Springs, loaded the bike on the trailer, and we returned to Warsaw. A few weeks later, as we were planning our return home, he again offered to haul my bike back to Texas along with his bike. Unfortunately, before our departure, the trailer developed mechanical problems, and he was not able to leave Warsaw at the same time we were. I was left with no option but to ride my bike home, fly back to Warsaw by commercial airline, load up Sandy and the pups, and then drive back to Texas. Riding alone from Missouri to Texas, I made the 1112-mile trip in three days without incident.

After returning home, Spartan Club president Heckman, presented me with a special commemorative patch for my biker vest, which read: ***"1000 Mile Solo Ride"***. Mike had recently joined the Harlingen Elks Lodge where we would often meet for a drink and relive our crazy days as *"Spartan Cruisers"*. Mike and his wife Deneen, and Sandy and I remain close friends to this day. We spent the next several years biking and owning several different models. After surviving several "close calls" on bikes, I finally realized riding motorcycles is for the younger dare devils, especially after we laid our bike over on a ride, breaking Sandy's ankle, which required surgery to insert 6 stainless screws to repair it. After that incident, I sold the bike and retired my vest which had been adorned over the years with numerous patches. My favorites reads – "Old age ain't for sissies".

(Sandy and Brian with their Harley-Davidson motorcycles)

In late 2019 my doctor sent me for a routine ultrasound scan on my stomach and kidneys. During the exam an abdominal aorta aneurysm (commonly referred to as an "AAA") was discovered. The scan revealed that the aneurysm was fractured and in danger of erupting. I was later told that when the abdominal artery ruptures, a person has about seven minutes before bleeding to death. I was referred to noted cardiologist, Dr. Shareef Hilmy, who immediately set me up for surgery. On November 10, on my 80th birthday, a stint was placed in my main abdominal aorta, removing pressure from the aneurysm and preventing a fatal loss of blood. The procedure was supposed to last for an hour; however, I was on the operating table for over five hours. Dr Hilmy later explained there had been a problem inserting the stint because of a blockage in the artery near the insertion point of my upper thigh. A cardiovascular surgeon was hurried to the operating room and inserted a bypass around the blockage, allowing the stint to be inserted into the artery. A few hours after the surgery, I was allowed to have visitors. One morning a distinguished gentleman came into my room and introduced himself as "Dr. Misick", the surgeon that had performed the bypass on my artery and asked how I was feeling. I immediately recognized the name and a familiar accent. I said, "I bet I know where you're from". Surprised, he asked, "And where would that be?" When I said, "The Turks & Caicos Islands", he had a startled expression. I explained that I had previously lived on Providenciales, and one of my best friends was a native Turks Islander named Washington Misick. Astonished, he smiled and replied, "That's my older brother!"

Just imagine! Here I am, in a hospital bed in Harlingen, Texas; 3000 miles from the Turks & Caicos Islands, after a life-threatening close call; and saved by the skills of a local cardiovascular surgeon, whose older brother was my close friend when I lived in the Turks & Caicos Islands 40 years earlier.

My **"Journey"** can't get any more **"Incredible"** than that.

EPILOGUE

Since that time, I have slowed down considerably. We sold the bikes, planes, and the Missouri house. Now in my eighties, and after sixteen years in the three-thousand-foot Harlingen home, I decided it was getting to difficult and expensive to maintain. In 2019 we sold the big house and moved to Cottonwood Creek Country Club, a gated retirement community closer to our doctors and shopping. I renewed an earlier interest in golf and began playing with other homeowners. Singing and playing music was another hobby I enjoyed over the years. When I was a teenager, I learned to play the steel guitar, 6-string guitar, and the 5-string banjo. Along with two other musician friends from the Harlingen Elk Lodge, we formed a local country band called "Yesterday's Wine", playing weekly at the Harlingen Elks Lodge, and other venues in the area for about 5 years.

However, amateur radio still remains my primary hobby. I have been a member of the Waterway Radio & Cruising Club Net for over sixty years. The Net meets daily, seven days a week, helping fellow amateur radio operators on boats with weather, navigational and safety information, especially during hurricane season. The Net coordinates with the US Coast Guard in search and rescue operations when a boater is missing or overdue at his destination. Most days I can be found either on the radio, playing golf, reading a book, or like for the past seven months, writing this one. I hope you have enjoyed reading my story. I would love to hear back from each of you, and your thoughts on *"Incredible Journey"*.

ACKNOWLEDGMENT

The motivation to write this book was the result of suggestions from many people who knew me personally. The biggest thanks goes to my wife Sandy for her support and patience for the many hours I was AWOL holed up in a small closet, writing this book. A very special thank you goes to Gary and Florence Wegan for convincing me to tell my story and volunteering their time to critique the writing. Your commitment and friendship is indeed a blessing. This book would never have happened without each of you.

Brian Hunsaker, May 2024.

Printed in the United States
by Baker & Taylor Publisher Services